GLACIER TRAVEL & CREVASSE RESCUE

GLACIER TRAVEL & CREVASSE RESCUE

SECOND EDITION

ANDY SELTERS

▶ READING GLACIERS

▶ TEAM TRAVEL

▶ CREVASSE RESCUE
  TECHNIQUES

▶ ROUTEFINDING

▶ EXPEDITION SKILLS

THE
MOUNTAINEERS

Published by
The Mountaineers
1001 SW Klickitat Way, Suite 201
Seattle, WA 98134

First edition, 1990. Second edition, 1999.

Published simultaneously in Great Britain by Cordee, 3a DeMontfort Street, Leicester, England, LE1 7HD

Manufactured in the United States of America

Edited by Brenda Pittsley
Illustrations by Jennifer Hahn
All photographs by the author except as noted
Cover and book design by Jennifer Shontz
Layout by Nick Gregoric

Cover photograph: *Crevasse rescue workshop on Mount Shasta, California* ©Ace Kvale (Front);
Michael Graber on Yerupajá, Peru ©Andy Selters (Back)

Frontispiece: *Crevasse self-rescue practice, Mount Shasta, California* ©Ace Kvale

Library of Congress Cataloging-in-Publication Data
Selters, Andrew.
    Glacier travel and crevasse rescue / Andy Selters. — 2nd ed. p. cm.
    Includes bibliographical references and index.
    ISBN 0-89886-658-8 (pbk. : alk. paper)
    1. Snow and ice climbing. 2. Snow and ice climbing—Safety measures. 3. Mountaineering—Search and rescue operations. I. Title.
  GV200.3 .S45 1999
  796.52'2'0289—dc21
                                            99-6454
                                             CIP

 Printed on recycled paper

CONTENTS

ACKNOWLEDGMENTS

I inherited the concept of this book from Dave Bishop, former guide for the North Cascades Alpine School. In the many years and many revisions since Dave left the project for medical school, a number of others have helped me develop this text. Of those, Brian Okonek of Alaska-Denali Guiding provided valuable information from the standpoint of an expert in Alaskan mountaineering. Others who helped were my coworkers at the American Alpine Institute; John Schutt offered an especially wide range of helpful suggestions, glaciologist Ron Johnson added his expertise to the hazard evaluation chapter, and Jill Fugate helped edit early drafts. Steve Boyer, Tom Dickey, Bruce Hendricks, Mark Houston, Alan Kearney, Dr. Eric Larson, Lance Machovsky, and Robert Parker all had answers to various queries, as did pack maker Rick Lipke of Skagit Mountain Rescue. I also appreciated learning new information about glaciers in Sue Ferguson's book *Glaciers of North America* (1992), which enhanced my thinking about the natural history of glaciers. Finally, thanks to Jennifer Hahn for her patience and creativity in developing the illustrations.

INTRODUCTION

"Man has evolved while the great continental ice sheets have waxed and waned through time, and he still has many lessons to learn in the art of living with the ice."

— Brian John.
The Ice Age Past and Present.

This is a manual for traveling over the white lands, the mountains, and high latitudes where the snowpack never melts away. These lands cover about 10 percent of the earth's surface and contain about 98 percent of our planet's fresh water. In these places where billions of tons of accumulated snow and ice entrain downhill, any travel is an adventure into raw beauty and intrinsic hazards.

When European cultures started taking geographic and personal quests into the mountains two and three hundred years ago, glaciers inspired as much or more fascination than even the peaks that surround them. From weaving over the Mer de Glace to discovering the Colorado pocket glaciers, early alpinists and tourists marveled at the rivers of accumulated snowflakes melded into flexing towers, popping fissures, groaning walls, and silent source fields. How incredible to walk over the back of something so huge and moving, almost alive! By the early 20th century a preliminary understanding of the major role glaciers have played in shaping mountains and even continents became widespread, and so appreciation of glaciers as awesome geology in action contributed much to the modern vision of a dynamic and ancient planet.

Nowadays we look more to the summits, often traveling over glaciers as a means of access. But glaciers hide crevasses, and avoiding a cold death in one of these hollows is a surprisingly technical problem unique to glacier travel. Although crossing a deceptively smooth glacier surface isn't usually compared with the drama of high-angle climbing, the person who breaks into a crevasse arrives suddenly in an utterly vertical world.

◀ *Party crossing South Cascade Glacier on Ptarmigan Traverse, North Cascades*

He or she may face a demanding extrication, one for which a winter climb of El Capitan might have been better preparation than a dozen previous uneventful glacier excursions. Therefore, having the savvy to avoid crevasses and the skill to rescue oneself or a partner from one when necessary are unpublicized but challenging and important aspects of mountaineering. At the very least, glacier-travel and crevasse-rescue skills foster an authentic confidence to venture farther. For those who travel glaciers frequently, these skills save lives.

While it's important to have a repertoire of skills, a party's safety and efficiency still depend on the attitudes of its members. Ideally, glacier travelers adopt an attitude that balances a healthy fear of crevasses with a cautious confidence in their own judgment and skills. Too often, however, an imbalance of attitudes either puts people in danger or causes them to fuss with barely relevant rigamarole. On one side are apparently naive climbers, from novice to experienced, who have thus far avoided a significant crevasse plunge and are prone to treat crevasses rather lightly. These people need to think through the reality of a crevasse fall and understand that slack procedures and rudimentary rescue skills will fail them in a real test.

On the other side are rule-conscious climbers who put their confidence in a combination of rigid procedures and safety in numbers. This attitude overlooks the dynamic of rope team plus glacier, and it fails to heighten skills, techniques, or intuition—all of which build genuine confidence and make glacier travel safer, more efficient, and more enjoyable.

With increased glacier mileage, a climber's attitude often progresses in an opposite manner from say, rock climbing. On trustworthy rock, climbers build their skills and strength and come to depend on their own expertise. With practice, they can climb confidently with less protection. But on glaciers, experience with crevasses typically amounts to numerous incident-free trips punctuated by terrifying and eye-opening surprises. Just one or two serious incidents may occur in a decade of glacier travel, but one or two are enough to deepen respect for the unpredictability and seriousness of the crevasse hazard. Thus, the common pattern is for seasoned climbers to become *more* reliant on their backup systems than they were when they were first learning.

Whatever degree of safety you hope for (and degree of risk you accept), you will of course strive to bring your procedures in line with those hopes. For some time, however, "common practices" did not meet reasonable expectations. From anchors to harnesses, from haul systems to judging snow, the general body of knowledge in glacier travel did not

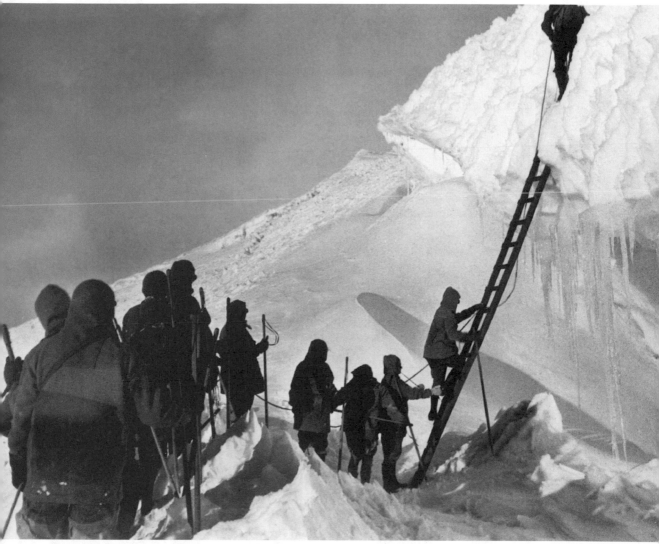

Party using a ladder to surmount a crevasse wall on Mount Rainier in the 1920s
(Courtesy U. S. National Park Service)

keep up with other advances in climbing. Especially little thought was given to the added risks of today's more demanding expeditions: small parties, heavy packs, hauling with sleds, and traveling on large, remote glaciers with rotten snow conditions.

While advances in awareness and technique have made glacier travel safer and more efficient, they can never attain perfection, so each

"…we made our way over masses of ice connected by shaky bridges of almost loose snow, most of which were either broken or incomplete. All of us broke through more than once, but by the careful use of the rope no accident occurred. Through the great holes with jagged margins produced by these stumbles, we saw mysterious azure caverns deep below, of the most marvelous blue ever created by snow, with a sheen like watered silk, and brilliant, almost metallic reflections."

—Filippo de Filippi, 1897.
The Ascent of Mount St. Elias.

traveler must make compromises according to personal comfort levels. In this book, enough procedure is described to satisfy the safety conscious, and those who are more interested in speed can compromise as they wish.

In that sense, this book should not be considered a catalog of rules, but rather a reference on which to build your own experiences. Also, discussion and controversy regarding glacier travel should continue, because refinements in technique will result. While this guide integrates techniques from climbers around the world, a bias toward the techniques familiar to the Pacific Northwest region of the United States is inevitable. Readers are presumed to have basic mountaineering skills, particularly the basic knots and techniques for ice-ax arrest, rappelling, and belaying. Beginners can find these skills described in a general mountaineering text, and should seek competent instruction in them.

In any case, as with any physical skill, reading by itself does not produce proficiency. Glacier-travel problems are impromptu engineering problems, with materials and time crucially limited and no certainty of the forces involved. The keys to competence are snow savvy, practice in roped travel and rescue techniques, a constant, critical evaluation of situations, and a bit of a sixth sense. These can be achieved only through applying "book knowledge" to years of excursions and to mock (or actual) rescues. Therefore, beginners and those of intermediate experience are especially warned to err on the side of caution whenever there is a question.

The most fundamental principle underlying this book is that any party on a glacier must assume that, in a mishap, either they themselves will be the rescuers or there will be no rescue. Accepting total self-sufficiency is the best possible incentive to be competent and prepared; it's also a responsibility to organized rescue teams and nearby parties who may or may not be available in time to risk their own goals and lives in a rescue. Thus, the bottom line reads that self-sufficiency is a responsibility. And after all, being self-sufficient in the mountains is really the essence of the "freedom of the hills."

A NOTE ABOUT SAFETY

Safety is an important concern in all outdoor activities. No book can alert you to every hazard or anticipate the limitations of every reader. The descriptions of techniques and procedures in this book are intended to provide general information. Nothing substitutes for formal instruction, routine practice, and plenty of experience. When you follow any of the procedures described here, you assume responsibility for your own safety. Use *Glacier Travel and Crevasse Rescue* as a general guide to further information. Under normal conditions, excursions into the backcountry require attention to traffic, road and trail conditions, weather, terrain, the capabilities of your party, and other factors. Keeping informed on current conditions and exercising common sense are the keys to a safe, enjoyable outing.

— The Mountaineers

Finding a way through an icefall on Mount Siniolchu, Sikkim Himilaya, India (Courtesy Ace Kvale)

CHAPTER 1

UNDERSTANDING THE CREVASSE HAZARD

Glaciers vary widely in the number of crevasses they hide, and their surface conditions change constantly. Therefore, the danger of breaking through a snowbridge into a crevasse ranges from negligible to very high, depending on the glacier and its condition. Just leaving camp on an Alaskan glacier in bad conditions can be riskier than climbing for two days on a typical alpine glacier. On the other hand, occasional treacherous conditions can make an alpine glacier just as dangerous as one in Alaska.

Obviously, one would like to know just how hazardous a given place is at a given time. However, beyond recognizing obvious open crevasses, "knowing" the crevasse hazard generally amounts to making educated guesses and using intuition. The starting point for making your guesses more educated and your intuition more practiced is to understand the origins of glaciers and crevasses.

GLACIER AND CREVASSE GENESIS

Glaciers form in the world's high, cold places where, during the average year, more snow falls than can melt away. Decade after decade the snow piles on top of itself. As it does so, it compresses the old, deeply buried layers, compacting them and squeezing air out. When the snow is compressed to about 80-percent solid, the remaining air pockets lose their connections and the snow becomes ice. This transition from snow to ice takes only a few years in a temperate area, maybe 15 years in colder regions, and more than 100 years on polar glaciers. Often you can see the layering of annual accumulations on a glacier's walls, like the annular rings in a tree stump. Each year's autumn surface stands out with ice from melt and dust from the atmosphere. Eventually the accumulation of snow and ice grows massive enough to sag and slide downhill. Compressed ice being in motion distinguishes a glacier from a snowfield.

Continuously fed by the deepening snows at a glacier's head, glacier ice creeps and glides down to lower elevations where temperate summers reduce it to melt-water. Thus, geologists often look at glaciers as gravity driven systems that dissipate "excess" snowfall. The upper area, where more snow falls than can melt away, is called the **accumulation zone**. The lower area, where accumulated ice that has moved down from above melts away, is called the **ablation zone**. In late summer and autumn when a year's melting is nearly complete, you can often easily distinguish the white, still-snowy, accumulation zone from the old, blue-gray ice of the ablation zone.

For an active glacier of average or smaller size in the Cascades or the Alps, it takes about 100 years for snow that fell in an accumulation zone to emerge as melting ice at a glacier's snout. Glaciers in very cold regions move slower, so for large, sub-polar glaciers this "turnover" can take more than 1,000 years.

Glacier ice behaves much differently than the rigid, brittle stuff of cocktail parties and hockey rinks. In response to the heavy pressure of tons of more recent ice and snow weighing on them, ice crystals deform, and molecules are shuttled from one crystal to the next. This process is called recrystallization. Acres of recrystallization result in "creep," causing glacier ice to flow almost like viscous lava, speeding and stretching, slowing and pooling, turning and flexing with the terrain. Glaciers also glide on their bedrock, especially when there is melt-water to lubricate their bellies. Warmth speeds both creep and glide, so temperate glaciers move up to fifteen times faster in summer than they do in winter. Overall, surface movement on a typical temperate glacier averages about a foot per day, or over 100 meters a year. About two-thirds of this motion comes from creep and one-third from glide.

Although the majority of super-compressed ice within a glacier can ooze across the terrain, the ice closer to the surface is more brittle. So when moving ice strains over bedrock features, the brittle surface splits. These splits in the glacier's surface are crevasses.

Crevasses are formed by tension created within the overall flow when some ice moves faster than ice around it. The most obvious **tension zone** is where ice flows over a sharply angled slope. This situation is similar to air flowing over a wing, in that the surface ice has farther to travel than the ice at the bedrock. The surface ice therefore accelerates over the steeper drop, and this "differential flow," plus the brittleness of surface ice, causes the ice to split.

This simple sort of tension zone creates **transverse crevasses,** slots that form perpendicular to the glacier's flow. A smooth drop will make a series of parallel crevasses form from a bit above the drop-off to somewhere above the bottom. In theory, crevasses at the bottom of the drop-off are sealed shut by the pooling, compressive flow; this area is known as a **compression zone** (see fig. 1.1).

Crevasse-forming tension also occurs when a glacier's margins drag and press against the adjacent mountain slopes and valley walls. Here, the center of a glacier is less affected—the central stream of ice courses on faster and more freely, as with the leading arm of an amoeba. This condition subjects the glacier's margins to two forces: compression from the adjoining rock and tension from the faster, central stream. These forces combine to create a classic pattern of herringbone crevasses angling up-glacier at 45 degrees, as shown in figure 1.2. These are called **marginal crevasses**. Usually the flow differential is greater toward the central end of marginal crevasses; therefore, they tend to widen toward the free-flowing center of the glacier.

Turns generate tension as well. The ice on the outside of a turn has farther to travel, and thus is pulled with tension creating **radial crevasses**. Ice along the inside edge suffers a confusion of tensions from all sides and can break into crisscross crevasses. Similar confusion results when glaciers with different drainages converge. Compressive forces from the merging flows create pressure that on the one hand seals crevasses but also creates pressure that speeds the flow and generates crevasses nearby.

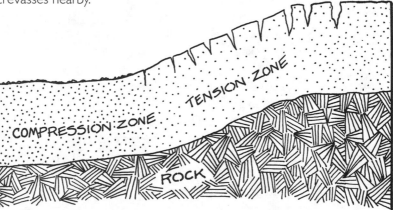

Figure 1.1 Cross-section of tension and compression zones

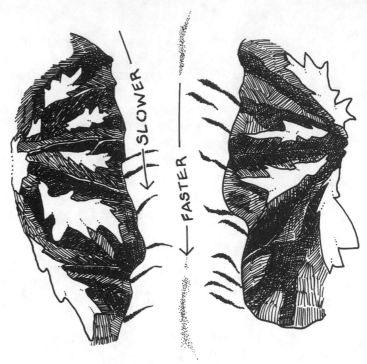

Figure 1.2 Marginal crevasses (top view)

In heavily glaciated regions like the Alaska Range, the tops of ridges can accumulate enough snow and ice to initiate flow off either side of the ridge line, creating a tension zone atop the ridge. Thus, crevasses can form along broad, relatively flat ridges. Those used to windswept ridge tops in a moderately glaciated region like the Cascades never expect to see crevasses here. In an analogous situation, the perennial cornices along ridge tops in heavily glaciated terrain can teeter downslope at glacial slowness, leaving shallow crevasses as they slowly crack away from the ridge line.

Finally, there is the uppermost crevasse in a glacier, the **bergschrund** (see fig. 1.3). This is the gap where the glacier pulls away from stationary ice and snow above. Above most bergschrunds, there rises a steep mountain headwall that sloughs off most snowfall; headwalls are generally too steep to collect enough mass to become part of the moving glacier. Because of all the snow that fills in from the headwall above, bergschrunds generally aren't as deep as normal crevasses, although they can be enormously wide and long.

Late summer travel on the Coleman Glacier, Mount Baker, North Cascades ▶

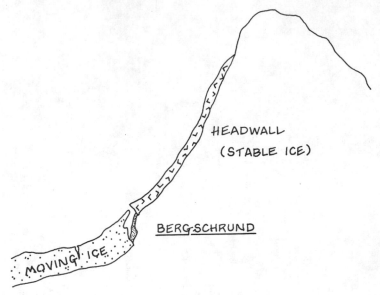

Figure 1.3 Cross-section of a bergschrund

Cousins to crevasses, **moats** are the melt-gaps between a glacier's edge and its surrounding rock walls. Moats can be fatally deep and over-hung by weak snow just like crevasses. Moats often run deeper than expected, because the adjacent rock warms in the sun, channeling heat and melt-water down to deepen the hole. Moats can be the most dangerous feature of small glaciers and snowfields like those in the Sierra or Tetons. Rock anchors often must be placed to belay across a moat.

Most crevasses are generally linear, extending perpendicular to the tension in the ice. They range from incipient slits to gigantic chasms capable of swallowing entire neighborhoods. Larger, thicker glaciers and the colder glaciers of the polar regions have larger and deeper crevasses. Small glaciers, in say the southern Cascades, may have crevasses no more than 15 feet across. The big glaciers in Alaska and the Karakoram have yawning gaps of up to 75 feet across. Even though legends abound of terrifying slots hundreds of feet deep, a crevasse on a temperate glacier is almost never deeper than 115 feet (30 meters). Polar glaciers generate crevasses up to 165 feet deep (50 meters). Because the plasticity of ice increases with depth, and because flow tension decreases with depth, crevasses tend to narrow gradually from the surface downward. Thus, getting tightly wedged is a common hardship to those who fall into crevasses.

Depending on its temperature and flow rate, glacier ice splits partly in slow deformation and partly in distinct lurches. A 6-foot-wide crevasse may open over the period of a couple months, widening an inch or so at a time, mostly in small but audible "ice quakes." Temperate glaciers form crevasses with a moderate percentage of recrystallization flow, whereas brittle polar glaciers pop and shudder constantly (see fig. 1.4).

The more active a glacier, the more crevasses it generates, so that small, stagnating glaciers essentially are snowfields with a bergschrund and a crevasse or two, while active sections of large glaciers might have more

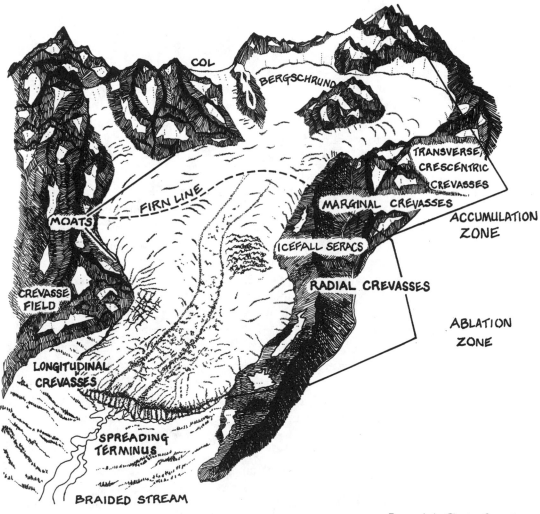

Figure 1.4 Glacier Overview

crevasses than solid ground in between. Many glaciers spill over cliffs or very steep sections, and here the ice periodically calves off in hunks of various proportions. The resulting chaos of crevasses and towers (called **seracs**) is known as an **icefall**.

This outline gives us a general idea of glacier flow and how crevasses form, but, as with fluid studies in general, science has never fully comprehended the dynamics of glaciers. Combinations of dropping, turning, dragging, colliding, pooling, and so on can create crevasses angling in any direction. Also, a glacier's flow often deforms crevasses as it carries them out of their original tension zone. Whatever the combined forces, however, they tend to be sustained over a given area, and, therefore, it's normal to find crevasses running fairly parallel within that area.

SNOWBRIDGES

The previous discussion can give the glacier traveler an abstract idea of where crevasses are most likely to be found, but it's the snow that bridges crevasses that makes them dangerous. Thus, the most important clues to assessing the crevasse hazard are a sharp eye for the dips and extensions of snowbridges, and an understanding of and subtle feel for the changing strength of the snow underfoot.

One characteristic of snow is that it tends to stick together. The "glue" is simply tiny necks of ice that freeze the individual crystals into an intricate network. When snow falls on a crevassed glacier, instead of dribbling into the crevasses like sand through a sieve, many of the crystals accrete on the crevasse lips, especially if the temperature is not far below freezing and if there is a wind. In this way cornices build out from the edges, and eventually they meet and partially or entirely bridge the crevasse. Also, during a storm season, continuing snowfall keeps the gaps bridged even as they widen with glacial movement.

When snowbridges are strong, they allow mercifully straightforward travel over crevasse-riddled terrain. But when they're weak, they unexpectedly drop climbers into the crevasse's dark depths. Whether a bridge gives the boon of access or the bane of collapse depends partly on its thickness, but more on the strength of its bonding network. With the nearly infinite types of snow, from new-fallen powder to old wind crust, this bonding network can be amazingly strong or hopelessly weak. The interacting forces of temperature, humidity, solar radiation, wind, and the snow's own weight determine the characteristics of snow; so the strength of an undisturbed snowbridge is determined by its climatic history and the current weather.

Because of seasonal climate patterns, most snowbridges are temporary affairs. Generally, they form and thicken during a stormy season, then progressively collapse during a fair-weather season, the season that climbers naturally favor. Let's take a closer look now at the main processes affecting snow and, hence, snowbridges.

Newly fallen snow is rather weak, but as a rule the delicate crystals start to settle as soon as they land and the accumulated layer gradually strengthens. Compaction, sintering (the rounding of crystals with vapor transfer), and wind battering—collectively known as **age hardening**—all combine to consolidate intricate, individual snowflakes into small, rounded grains held together by stronger, more interconnected bonds (see fig. 1.5). This process goes on in temperatures below the melting point, although it slows to insignificance below -40 degrees Fahrenheit or

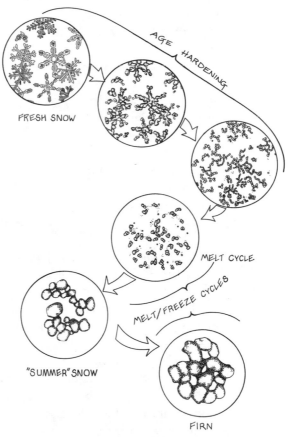

Figure 1.5 *Important processes of snow on a glacier*

so. By this process, snow can strengthen considerably within a couple of days to a couple of weeks after falling. Deeper snow compresses and strengthens itself more, so thicker snowbridges are stronger not only from their greater mass but also from a sturdier bonding network.

When this "new" (unmelted) snow warms to the melting point (generally in the spring), the bonding network quickly collapses. In the first thaws, the necks between crystals melt first, and the snow can swiftly deteriorate into an insubstantial slurry of crystals and melt-water. The low-density, dry snow of continental and subarctic regions has weaker bonds that break down faster and deeper than do those of the denser, wetter snow of maritime climates. But in any case, when the melt-water refreezes (generally at night) the bonds re-form more thickly, the crystals grow larger and rounder, and the whole network consolidates itself stronger than before. Typically what happens during late springtime then, is that daytime heat melts the snowbridges into weak slush and nighttime cold freezes them into strong "Styrofoam-snow" or **melt-freeze** snow. When the melt-freeze cycle continues for many weeks the snow gradually consolidates into very coarse-grained, very firm **"summer snow."** Late summer sun softens only the surface of this old snow, and even a plunging ice-ax shaft might penetrate just a few inches. Old snow that makes it through a full melt season and into the next one becomes a very dense, transitional snow-ice known as **firn**, or **névé**.

For the typical summer excursion, then, it can be invaluable to get a feel for the strength of snow after a period of melt-freeze cycles, and to continually assess the ongoing cycle each day.

Besides gauging the general snow conditions, climbers of course want to know exactly where the hidden crevasses lie. This is especially difficult when snowbridges are of "new" snow as the unmelted snow tends to cover a glacier's structure with a smooth, level blanket. But a bridge begins to sag after it goes through some melt-freeze cycles. These sags can become quite dramatic over time. Also, as spring progresses, low-lying sags tend to collect more dust. They also tend to collect more of the new powder from a late spring or summer dusting of snow. For these reasons, it's common to see snowbridges accentuated by dustier snow or, conversely, by cleaner, whiter snow.

Also, when snowbridges collapse they rarely do so all at once. Rather, sections of the bridge progressively melt and drop away, leaving a hole that hints at a wider and longer underlying crevasse. So when you see a hole in the glacier's surface it's wise to assume there's a crevasse extending well beyond the visible abyss, especially lengthwise.

Climbers on Yerupajá Glacier, Cordillera Huayhuash, Peru

Even though crevasses often exhibit visual clues as to their existence, many do not. The history of mountaineering includes the obituaries of many who found this out the hard way. Prudent climbers assume that anywhere there's snow on a glacier, there might be a crevasse.

GLACIER SEASONS IN VARIOUS CLIMATES

Knowing the pattern of snow evolution, we can now generalize about the annual cycles of surface conditions on glaciers in various climates.

MARITIME, TEMPERATE CLIMATES

Most glacier travelers climb in temperate latitudes, where the mountains have generally winter-wet and summer-dry climates like the Cascades and the European Alps. Here most glaciers range in length from a mile or two to maybe 10 miles.

Typically, winter in the temperate latitudes is characterized by a westerly storm track that buries glaciers with deep snowfall. Mountain slopes near the western coasts of the continents receive a particularly heavy load of wet, maritime snowfall. Slightly more continental, the Alps receive somewhat less winter snow than the Cascades. Aside from meaning a lot of poor weather for travel, the heavy snows of midwinter present glacier travelers with good news and bad news. The bad news is that most crevasses are undetectable under the deep, unmelted snow and since temperatures persist below the freezing point the snow cannot melt and refreeze into a stronger network. The good news is that although crevasses are hidden, most bridges become thick enough to bear plenty of weight. For this reason, most climbers consider middle to late winter to be a relatively safe time to travel in temperate regions, especially on skis (see fig. 1.6 for the complete snowbridge cycle).

This relative safety continues until sometime in the spring when long days, a high sun and warm air start melting the snowpack. Depending on the depth of the pack and the heat of the season, within a week or two the bridges start to sag and collapse, becoming quite unsafe. Strong sun makes snowbridges most dangerous in the afternoon and evening, with nighttime freezes bringing relative safety during the late night and early morning. But spring conditions can be especially treacherous if nighttime cloud cover or generally warm air keeps the snow from refreezing at night, so that the following day melt-water percolates much deeper into the snowpack and deteriorates the bridges that much more. Down in the ablation zone the spring thaw starts early, gradually progressing up the glacier as the season warms. This means that when the

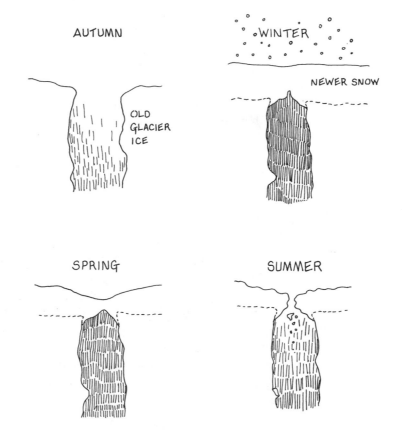

Figure 1.6 Typical snowbridge seasons on a temperate glacier

lower part of a glacier has its "spring," the upper reaches are still in "winter."

As spring turns to summer, the lengthening "melt" portion of the daily melt-freeze cycle collapses many snowbridges, and the crevasses open up. After a few weeks of this cyclic decay, those bridges that persist withstand melt-weakening more and more and are more likely to remain firm into late morning or even midday. However, a late spring or early summer snowfall can rebridge the newly opened crevasses with a scanty and treacherous few inches of new snow. Summer snowfalls are common in the cooler, higher elevations of the Pennine and Bernese Alps and many bridges persist through the season. Overall, though, warm summer weather on a temperate glacier gradually opens the crevasses, leaving fewer, but more trustworthy, snowbridges. By late September, there might not be a single snowbridge left on a Cascade glacier, and the primary challenge of travel can be to wend a route through mazes of wide-open crevasses.

As temperatures drop, autumn snowfalls dangerously veil open crevasses with a thin layer of powder. As little as 4 or 5 inches of new snow can lay an even, white blanket that obscures all signs of crevasses, but of course this snow will not support the most featherweight climber. It is almost a certainty at this time that any bridge or overhang will give way. Further, it can be very difficult to stop a partner's crevasse fall because the hard summer surface underneath can be quite difficult to ice-ax arrest on, and a stiff crevasse edge will slow the rope very little (see the chapters on travel and rescue techniques). When conditions are like this, it's wise to just stay off glaciers. The snow accumulations of late fall and early winter, though, make it easier to hold a partner's fall, then gradually stack the bridges high enough to bear weight, bringing a return to the relative safety of midwinter.

The temperate glaciers of the Southern Hemisphere—found in the New Zealand Alps and Patagonia—form in a stormier climate than do those of the Northern Hemisphere. Thus, Patagonia has the two largest temperate **icecaps** (large "icefields" where a plateau of ice sends off flow in all directions) in the world, even though the latitude is similar to that of southern British Columbia, and the peak altitudes are similar to those of the North Cascades. Some glaciers in both New Zealand and Patagonia extend more than 20 miles. Austral summers are not frigid, however, so the accumulation zones in both regions collect rain as well as snow. This means that snowbridges cycle through degrees of sloppiness throughout the summer.

SUBARCTIC CLIMATES

Typified by those in the Alaska Range, subarctic glaciers have the always-frozen characteristics of polar glaciers in their upper reaches, while their ablation zones are temperate, with melt-water and moderate temperatures easing their flow. The Alaska Range has very large glaciers, many over 30 miles long. These glaciers receive much of their snow in the late summer and early fall, which means that crevasses can be fairly well covered as the bitter, but relatively dry winter moves in. The dry, intense cold of winter keeps these bridges from strengthening as much as on temperate glaciers. In subarctic climates, it's mostly wind that age-hardens the snow during the winter; exposed spots become stiff with a few inches of "wind board." Pockets protected from the wind remain powdery into the spring thaw.

When thawing temperatures arrive in April, May, or June depending on the elevation, the subarctic days are so long that melt-water suddenly percolates well into the snowpack, making it deeply treacherous for weeks. The bridges, built of cold, light snow and suddenly infused with melt-water, can show little or no sag or stress, and even surprisingly thick ones can readily collapse, especially in the warm afternoons. As a result, climbers in the Alaska Range fall through far more frequently and more unexpectedly than do climbers on temperate glaciers.

Midsummer opens the crevasses and deteriorates bridges with appalling speed, but firmer, more-trustworthy bridges usually don't develop, because occasional or frequent snowfalls keep renewing them with untrustworthy snow. This oscillation between thawing temperatures and accumulating snow sets up ideal conditions to prolong instability. Like any glacier condition, this prolonged instability moves up-glacier with the advance of the season, and so unstable bridges are a serious problem somewhere on the giant Alaskan glaciers throughout the spring and summer. Moderate to severe instability can persist until the colder days and heavier snows of late summer and autumn rebuild the bridges to relative strength.

The subarctic glaciers of southeastern Alaska and western Yukon form under a similar, but more maritime regime. The combination of high peaks near the coast in a strong storm track makes for incredible snowfalls—30 feet can fall in a week, even in May—and the "winter" accumulation season is some 10 months long. The result is the third most extensive glacial terrain on the planet after Antarctica and Greenland. Glaciers here are seas of ice up to 15 miles wide and 90 miles long that fill great valleys with ice more than 1,500 feet deep. There are also large icefields. The usual climbing season, April through July, starts out bitterly cold but quickly warms, with thawing conditions progressing above 10,000 feet by the summer solstice.

CONTINENTAL CLIMATES

The Canadian Rockies and the eastern European Alps (Bergalia and Tyrol) typify a continental climate: very cold in the winter, with snowfalls that can come any time of year. The winters often bring only modest snowfall—just a few feet or less of dry powder—and, therefore, crevasse bridges can remain barely substantial into the early spring. But storms usually pass through from March through May, building bridges as the temperature gradually warms. Then, as in a maritime summer, melt-freeze cycles can alternately deteriorate and reinforce the snowbridges, or 24-hour melting temperatures can just weaken them. Snowfall and rain are common too, keeping bridges relatively soggy and treacherous, especially at higher elevations. September typically brings an early onset of cold air and more stable (although quite broken) glacier surfaces, until occasional storms bridge the fairly open slots with light powder.

POLAR REGIONS

The cold, dry climates of the polar regions generate glacier ice that almost never melts. The interior of places like Ellesmere and Baffin islands, Greenland, and Antarctica may receive only a few inches of snowfall each year. But so little of this ever melts that these regions are mostly vast icecaps, by far the most extensive glacier terrain on the planet. Ice in Antarctica and Greenland accounts for a huge majority of the world's fresh water.

Occasional warm summer days melt the surface some, but the overall mass of ice and polar temperatures assure that most of the melt-water only refreezes. Over centuries, this has created super-hard ice. In the extreme polar deserts you find light amounts of new snow blowing over glazed ice as old as civilization and as hard as granite. The sharpest ice screws and ice tools penetrate this stuff only under heavy persuasion. In these conditions, few snowbridges are strong enough to be trust-worthy, though the ice is less active in these dry areas and so there are fewer crevasses. The most dangerous regions get a moderate amount of snow, enough to generate crevasse-forming motion and weak bridges.

SUBTROPICAL AND TROPICAL GLACIERS

The very high and extensive mountains of the Himalaya and the Andes have a wide range of climates. In general, the high altitude and high-angle sun of these mountains bring snow conditions that can fool a climber used to temperate glaciers. Snow deteriorating under an intense sun in the very dry air does not always turn slushy; rather, the moisture subli-mates or evaporates. The snow structure weakens by becoming more airy and "rotten," without the telltale sogginess of warm snow at temper-ate latitudes. Also, the intense radiation exaggerates the difference be-tween north- and south-facing slopes.

The glaciers of Nepal typically extend from steep accumulation zones to 15 miles or more down the valley. The long ablation zones are covered with rock rubble that has fallen off the adjacent slopes. Hiking here can be a difficult stumble over debris that slides on the ice.

Two distinct seasons feed these glaciers. From June to early Sep-tember, the summer monsoons dump a lot of relatively wet snow at the higher elevations, and from late December through March winter storms drop moderate amounts of cold, dry snow. During both the pre- and post-monsoon climbing seasons, melt-freeze conditions prevail and gradually open the crevasses. The surprisingly warm pre-monsoon season, right after winter's colder snowfall, can make for especially treacherous bridges. Somewhat cooler and shorter days in the post-monsoon season make the opening-up process more gradual. New snow can rebridge crevasses anytime during the two climbing seasons, especially pre-monsoon.

Farther northwest in the Himalayan chain, in the Karakoram, the monsoon season has little effect and the continental climate brings snowfall any time of year. The very high elevations attract much more precipitation overall than in other continental ranges, however, and the winters are much longer and colder than in Nepal. So here flow the greatest temperate glaciers in the world, with many over 30 miles long. As in Nepal, the long ablation zones convey vast quantities of fallen rock. The big accumulation zones have proportionately large crevasses.

Spring and summer bring searing hot days, but the nights chill rapidly in the thin atmosphere. Therefore, radical temperature swings induce radical melt-freeze cycles throughout the climbing season. Unfortunately, periodic storms between clear spells usually add fresh snowfall, and so the accumulation zones of the Karakoram can be as treacherous as those in Alaska.

The Andes of Peru and Bolivia have glaciers of a more alpine scale, from 3 to 10 miles long. The climate here is markedly seasonal. The high-sun "winter" (September/October through March/April) brings easterly trade winds with snow virtually every day, while the low-sun "summer" climbing season (May through August) brings daily clear skies with occasional afternoon squalls. Intense melt-freeze cycles are quite predictable during "summer," and the onset of the season gradually opens but strengthens the glacier surfaces. In these conditions, melt-water freezes into sub-surface ice, and so bridges can be even stronger than they might look to a temperate climber. Bridges sag less than in temperate regions, however, so they're less visible under snow. When an icy bridge gets old and "honey-combed" the ice can fail unexpectedly. The chance of snowstorms rebuilding soft bridges decreases farther south, and in Bolivia the dry season is particularly long and pronounced.

HEALTH OF GLACIERS

Glaciers depend on lots of snowfall for their "health," and so their condition fluctuates with the climate. Even though numerous glaciers have advanced in recent decades, the twentieth century has been one of general glacial reduction almost everywhere in the world. Most glaciers in the Cascades and the Alps have thinned and receded. High routes that went over smooth glacial terrain in the 1950s are now complex with crevasses and seracs, or even require rock climbing.

The ancestors of the Baltis of the Karakoram drove pack animals over glacier passes to trade in Central Asia, but with thinner glaciers those trade relations are blocked by icefalls and rock cliffs. Andean ice faces climbed in the 1960s are thinning to remnant seracs calving over rock buttresses, and Patagonia's glaciers are now miles shorter than they were just a couple decades ago. Near British Columbia's Mount Sir Sandford, in a spot where glacier ice ran 200-feet thick in 1900, a hut now stands in a meadow with a distant glacier view.

Perhaps the most dramatic contemporary recession has been in southeast Alaska. Glaciers that mariner George Vancouver saw calving at the outer coast 200 years ago now end 100 miles inland, across now-open Glacier Bay. This retreat accelerated in the last quarter of the twentieth century, so maps of the coastal area made in 1971 were seriously out of date by 1990.

This general retreat started before the Industrial Revolution, but the possibility that much of the recession is caused by human-induced global warming is distressing. Once again, glaciers seem to be contributing to our view of the world and our place in it.

OPENINGS

As soon as classes let out for the summer following my freshman year in college, I headed for the north side of California's giant volcano, Mount Shasta. It was my first glacier climb, and I was lucky to join two experienced partners. They gave me a middle knot to clip into along with instructions to keep the line snug as we traveled. We climbed a steep chute to the top on a blazing hot day, using "glacier cream" to hold our sunburns to the blister stage. I was thrilled with my first big summit and ready to take on more.

We were nearly back in camp, traveling on easy ground, when the guy up front seemed to fall to his knees. I paused, and the guy behind me shouted for me to get ready for a possible arrest. I laughed, thinking, "Yeah, right, he's really going to fall on a ten-degree slope." But it was no joke, and I got a reprimand. I had no idea what a crevasse was or why the leader had suddenly sunk into the ground. He struggled up and we got to camp.

When they explained to me that the surface of a glacier is hollow in places, my eyes grew wide. I cringed at the thought of plummeting into one of those icy black holes. There had been no sign of a trap where he had fallen, just smooth snow. Worse, they said that it's typical that if you fall in very far you can't just climb out, because the snow is loose and overhanging. Suddenly I had more questions than confidence, and I doubted the wisdom of going where we had just gone.

On the next trip, my primary goal was to rappel into a crevasse and practice ascending out. But even with that experience, the idea of hidden pitfalls anywhere bothered me so much I wondered if one shouldn't anchor-belay every step.

CHAPTER 2

PRINCIPLES AND PROCEDURES OF GLACIER TRAVEL

"[The crevasses] soon became more numerous and were ugly things to look into, much more so to cross. . . . The snow lay up to [the] edges and traveling became so insecure that we had to take to the ropes, and so, like a long chain of criminals, we wound our way along. In this mode we moved much faster, each man taking his run and clearing even broad crevasses if they crossed the direction we were traveling."

— Henry Haversham Godwin-Austen, on exploring the Karakoram for the Mustagh Pass, 1860. From *When Men and Mountains Meet*. John Keay.

It cannot be overstated how valuable it is to understand crevasses and snow if you hope to stay off weak snowbridges. But no one can judge snow perfectly, so the bottom line for the glacier traveler remains this: Where there's snow on a glacier there's a chance of plunging into a crevasse. It is impossible to say exactly how great this chance is, and the likelihood varies greatly with place and time. Therefore, with uncertainty presumed, partners on a snow-covered glacier travel roped together in order to stop each other's crevasse falls and to rescue each other. This chapter covers the procedures for travel, and the next two chapters cover rescue.

Roped travel sounds straightforward, but it takes coordinated, alert teamwork for a team to travel efficiently. And only thorough preparations can knit a realistic safety net—a simplistic "rope up and go" attitude

◀ *Descending a glacier on Imjatse, Khumbu Himal, Nepal*

provides only a false sense of security. The preparations and considerations might seem overwhelming to a beginner; to the naive they might seem like burdensome rigamarole. But the procedures become almost second nature after just a handful of excursions.

ARRANGING MEMBERS: HOW FAR APART?

Glacier travel teams function differently depending on the number of members, their experience, and how they arrange themselves on the rope(s). Other things being equal, a team's dynamic strongly correlates to how far apart members tie in, and thereby the distance between them as they travel. A greater distance between members means there's plenty of rope to span wide crevasses, little chance of one falling member pulling in another, and more freedom to negotiate corners and zigzags. However, greater distance between members also makes it easier to develop more slack between them, potentially enough to turn a trivial "punch in" into a fall that requires a rescue. A traditional distance to balance these factors for travel on small or medium glaciers is 30 to 60 feet apart. So with these trade-offs in mind, let's see how teams of two to five members work.

THREE-PERSON ROPE TEAMS

Having three people per rope, one on each end and one in the middle, has long been the accepted minimum for a glacier travel team because, assuming the members travel with care, it virtually assures that two people will be available to hold a fall and anchor the rope. With a 150-to-165-foot rope, this sets the members a relatively distant 75 to 80 feet apart. On an Alaskan or Karakoram-size glacier this distance is necessary to span large crevasses, but for smaller glaciers, particularly those with complex crevasse fields, it is wise to travel with shorter spans.

In general, a shorter span has less slack and crevasse falls will be shorter because of it. In crevasse fields, it is easier to keep shorter spans perpendicular to the crevasses (discussed in greater detail under "Team Travel" later in this chapter). To shorten the span, the end partners can each tie in 20 to 25 feet from the rope's end and carry the slack coiled and knotted over their shoulders, or use the kiwi tie-in described in Appendix 2. This "spare" rope also comes in handy during rescues.

Whether on a long or short span, teammates of differing abilities should arrange themselves so that the person who goes first is the one most practiced at routefinding and judging crevasses and the person with the least experience travels in the middle.

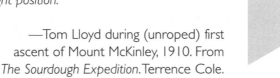

"…if you do fall in a small [crevasse] your pole will fall across the walls and hold you up if you carry it in the right position."

—Tom Lloyd during (unroped) first
ascent of Mount McKinley, 1910. From
The Sourdough Expedition. Terrence Cole.

FOUR- TO FIVE-PERSON ROPE TEAMS

A party of four or five can choose whether to travel on one rope or two. The advantages of the entire group traveling on one rope (one on each end and the others tied in evenly along its length) include more person-power to hold falls and less rope weight for each person to carry. In addition, if a party of four or five includes a couple of novices, it can be wise to "hide" them in the middle of a single, more populous rope than to "expose" them on the end of another rope.

A potential drawback of a team of four or five traveling on one rope is that it puts them closer together (less than 40 feet apart with five on a 165-foot rope). This adds some risk that two members instead of just one could end up in a slot. Moreover, a populous rope team will encounter more hassles, slower going, and sometimes more risk as the members turn corners, hop crevasses, pace themselves, and generally work to coordinate with one another. Finally, a party of four or five that divides itself into two rope teams can find that the second rope gives them more options in the event of a complicated rescue (see chapters 3 and 4).

In summary, if a glacier is relatively small with not many crevasses, a single rope for four or five provides a reasonable system. But if the glacier is large or in a broken condition, it's smart to split four or five members into two rope teams.

TWO-PERSON ROPE TEAMS

Should a party of four or five divide itself into two rope teams, at least one of those will be a two-person team, and that pair will depend on just one member to hold the other's crevasse fall. This is a reasonable chance to take in most cases (exceptions are discussed under "Holding Falls" later in this chapter), as unless a pair travels carelessly or in particularly dangerous conditions, a single climber should be able to resist the force generated by a crevasse fall. However, though a single climber can expect to *hold* a crevasse fall, for that single climber to *rescue* a fallen partner is another matter. Therefore, all but very experienced two-person rope teams will depend on help from another team in their party to at least anchor the rope should one of the pair break through a snowbridge. Consequently, a party with a two-person rope team should take extra care to keep another team reasonably nearby the roped pair.

A roped pair that is part of a multi-team party can tie in about one-third of the rope's length apart, giving each member an extra third of the rope to carry coiled and securely knotted around their shoulders. On large glaciers with particularly wide crevasses—for instance, the ones that are 50-to-60-feet wide in the Alaska and Karakoram Ranges—the pair can increase their distance from each other, carrying less "spare" rope but still ensuring they'll be able to span the wider slots.

TWO-PERSON PARTIES

To team up with just one partner on a glacier excursion calls for some serious thought. While it's not unreasonable to assume that each of the pair will be able to hold the other's crevasse falls, the two need to ask themselves if each can reasonably expect to then anchor the rope while holding the other's weight, and then extricate the partner. Because this prospect is too demanding to be realistic for many people, in the prudent days of yore no one ventured onto a snow-covered glacier in a party of fewer than three (or so the old-timers claim).

Today the climbing community tacitly approves of two-person parties, partly because better techniques and equipment make the prospect safer, but mostly because climbers are either willing to take more risk or don't realize the greater risk they take. In particular, the push to do more technical routes—where the most efficient team size is two—has put more solitary pairs on glaciers. Most climbers, if they think about it much, assume that they travel with the safety net of their partner anchoring them off and potentially rescuing them. However, although single-handed rescue is possible, relatively few climbers know how demanding it can be.

Assuming that two climbers are sufficiently competent, each member should tie in with enough spare rope to reach the other should he be dangling in a crevasse—tying in about 5 feet farther than one-third from an end will do the job. Thus, with a 165-foot rope, each member ties in at about 60 feet (one-third of 165 feet, plus 5 feet) from an end and carries this extra rope coiled and securely knotted over the shoulder; the pair travels with about 45 feet of rope between them. The actual footage can't be exact, of course, but it's wiser to err on the side of carrying more rope and having less rope between members, to ensure enough is available to reach each other.

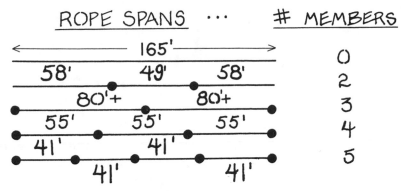

Figure 2.1 Recommended rope spans between team members

On the giant glaciers of subarctic zones and in the Karakoram, 45 feet of rope will not span many of the huge crevasses. Two-person parties going out alone on these glaciers should consider traveling either with a much longer rope or with two ropes. With two 165-foot ropes, each partner ties into one end of one rope, and about 75 feet from the end of the other rope. This leaves the partners 75 feet apart with 90 feet of extra rope to carry.

Figure 2.1 summarizes the recommended spans between members for rope teams of various sizes. An easy way to measure off tie-in locations for teams of any number is to count arm spans: With arms outstretched, the distance from fingertip to fingertip is nearly the same as the measurer's height, so the arm span of a 6-foot man is approximately 6 feet.

Crevasse falls rarely put a severe strain on a rope. It has long been accepted that approved "half ropes" of 9 millimeters (or even smaller diameters) are adequate for glacier travel.

SOLO GLACIER TRAVEL

Some of the greatest contemporary alpine climbers climb solo, unroped. It's said that great climbers know the crevasse hazard more intimately, so they are able to travel safely by carefully choosing when and where they go. This is true to some extent, but it's at least as true that these climbers simply are willing to take more risk. Unroped climbers generally cannot afford a single crevasse fall. While we can be impressed at the exploits of Reinhold Messner, he escaped a crevasse on Mount Everest only by sheer luck. The crevasse hazard finally caught up to the great solo climber Renatto Casarotto, and it has for other experienced solo climbers as well.

"Anyone who ventures alone on a snow-covered glacier, whatever his skill, is giving to everybody, except himself, a proof that he lacks the chief virtue of a mountaineer, judgement."

—Geoffrey Winthrop Young,
1946. *Mountaincraft.*

Some solo climbers travel with anchored **self-belay** systems. One such soloist en route to Alaska's Mount Huntington fell into a nasty crevasse. Although his system worked, it took him most of a day to extricate himself and his gear, and he gave up his attempted climb.

Other Alaskan soloists fix themselves to bridging systems. In the 1970s, Charlie Porter revived an old sourdough trick of traveling with a pole, in his case an aluminum one attached to his pack. The idea was that, if he fell in, the pole would bridge the crevasse and he would use it to clamber out. On a solo winter ascent of Denali, veteran climber Naomi Uemura attached two poles to his pack. Uemura never returned from this climb, but his recovered journal indicates that he fell into a crevasse at one point and the poles worked as intended.

Dave Johnston invented a more complex soloing apparatus called "Bridge-It." This was something like a ladder with skis on both ends; he'd walk or ski between the girders of this thing, dragging it along with the idea that, should he punch in, it would bridge the crevasse and he'd walk out on it. It also served as a sled to carry his load. Since then others have used ladders to solo on glaciers. A clear disadvantage is that in order to span a crevasse the ladder must be fairly perpendicular to the slot. In general, these and other soloing methods offer a sketchy and/or unwieldy backup to those who are committed to risky travel.

KNOTS AND HARNESSES

A person on the end of a rope should tie in directly to the harness, using a proven knot like the figure-eight retrace. Teammates along the rope's span can clip a figure eight on a bight or butterfly knot into a locking carabiner paired with a standard carabiner, then reversing the two gates.

Glacier travelers need to pay special attention to their harness systems, because crevasse falls often leave one dangling in free space for a long time. In this situation two criteria are crucial to survival: that your harness support you as comfortably as possible (don't laugh!) with as much surface area as possible, and that it keep you from hanging upside down. To these ends you'll want a harness with especially broad webbing or fabric, and one whose waistband cinches just *above* your hipbones, supporting you with a high center of gravity (see fig. 2.2). "Swami belt" tie-ins without leg loops should never be used as a climber dangling from one essentially hangs from the diaphragm and suffocates in minutes. Harnesses improvised from runner webbing constrict circulation and should be avoided.

The second criterion, prevention from hanging upside down, concerns the least-appreciated trauma of falling into a crevasse. Good preparation for anyone going out on a glacier is to hang from a tree upside down in a seat harness until your breathing falters and your head fills with blood and feels ready to explode. Tree-hanging is also a good test of a seat harness's center of gravity. If you need a lot of effort from your stomach muscles to hold yourself upright, your seat harness alone is inadequate.

If your seat harness supports you with a high center of gravity, if you're not wearing a pack, and if you don't plan on being knocked unconscious in a fall, then it is reasonable to expect that you can fall into a crevasse without tipping over. But if your harness doesn't really reach over

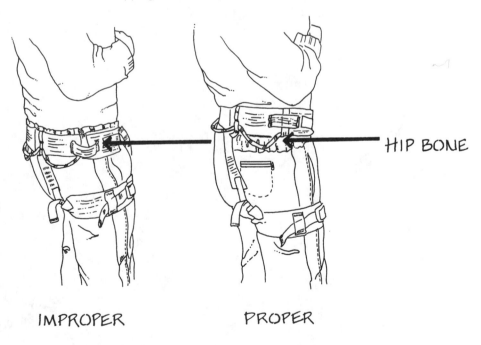

IMPROPER   PROPER   HIP BONE

Figure 2.2 Properly and improperly fitting waist harnesses

your hipbones, or if you're naturally top-heavy, and especially if you carry a pack much heavier than twenty pounds or so, then it's wise to use one of a few different methods to ensure you'll stay upright.

The tried and true method is to wear a **full-torso (body) harness**. Unfortunately, body harnesses have not caught on in the United States, so to get one you might have to special order one or take a trip to Canada or Europe.

The U.S. answer has been to wear a **chest harness** in conjunction with a seat harness. In serious falls, such as rock climbing leader falls, the two elements of this seat/chest system can compress together, bowing and potentially injuring the middle spine. But this is less of a concern for crevasse falls.

For those who choose a seat/chest system, an effective chest harness can be improvised with webbing and a carabiner (see fig. 2.3). Make sure that this harness fits quite snugly, and won't ride up around your neck. Notice how the rope runs only through the chest harness carabiner, holding the climber's body upright, but with his weight still bearing directly on the seat harness. *Never* knot the climbing rope to any chest harness because you'll end up hanging from it; at least one glacier traveler has been strangled this way. For a similar reason, make your seat-harness

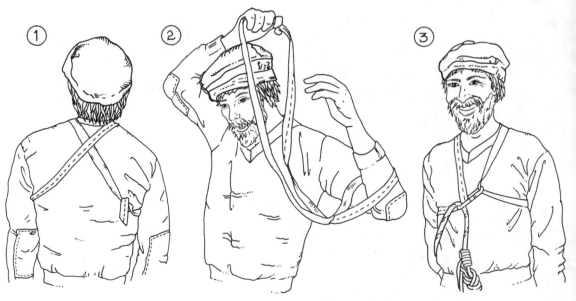

Figure 2.3 Improvising a chest harness

tie-in knot short, to be sure it doesn't reach up to the chest harness and jam into it before bearing on the seat harness.

If you're wearing a pack, another, somewhat untested, solution is to clip the climbing rope to a sturdy strap on the pack, at or just below shoulder level, but not where the rope will press against your neck in a fall (see fig. 2.4). In effect, this makes your pack work as a modestly effective chest harness, and a stiff pack may help eliminate the compression of seat/chest systems. With this in mind, pack manufacturers could build packs with extra-strong shoulder/sternum strap systems, or you can hitch a small length of webbing around one of the shoulder straps. Those roped between two partners will want to clip only one of the two strands leading from the harness. When you do end up in a crevasse with a pack on, this pack-clip method allows you to immediately jettison your pack onto the climbing rope. If you're already using a chest harness, you can still achieve this convenience by traveling with a runner on the pack clipped to the rope.

Yet another solution is to tie in with the kiwi coil system, which forms a modestly effective chest harness out of rope coils. (See Appendix 2.)

Any of these methods for keeping upright in a crevasse work against you when you need to hold a partner's crevasse fall. That is, to

Figure 2.4 Improvising a chest harness by clipping the rope to a pack strap

the degree that they support you upright on a free-hanging rope, they pull you headfirst toward a falling partner and hinder your ability to arrest with your ice ax. This is a serious concern, and for this reason some people advocate never tying in with anything but a seat harness. The controversy will never be settled, but case histories suggest that the risk of hanging upside down is somewhat more of a concern than that of trying to stop a fall while wearing a high-pull tie-in system. If you have three or four members on a rope, then you should be able to count on holding a fall regardless of your tie-in. The strongest point to make is that when you travel with a large pack on a glacier, it's smart to be extra cautious and to think even more carefully before you travel with just one partner.

In summary, if you're carrying no pack or only a light pack, tie in with just a seat harness. If you're carrying a heavy pack, I recommend tying in with one of the methods described here to help support your torso should you fall in.

CLOTHING

It's tough to climb in tropical temperatures and still be ready for an instant drop into a refrigerator, but often that's what glacier travel calls for. A reflecting glacier at altitude can be incredibly hot on a sunny summer day, but the temperature inside the crevasses remains around freezing or colder—hypothermia is one of the principal killers of crevasse victims. Having clothing handy in the pack is important, but too often a crevasse fall leaves the victim wedged or partly buried, and the pack is inaccessible.

The best answer is to wear clothing that ventilates. "Pit zips," knicker socks to roll down, full-zip wind pants, and synthetic insulation make for a clothing system that's comfortable in a wide range of temperatures. A valuable item for sunny days is a thick, white shirt that will reflect the sun yet still insulate in a crevasse. Also, it's easy to keep a warm hat handy to quickly insulate your head, the part of your body that loses more heat than any other. Finally, perhaps the most important concern is that your hands be ready for work inside a crevasse. Either overdress them or carry gloves or mittens very close by—on your wrists or harness or in a pocket.

RESCUE GEAR

The final preparation before a team heads onto a glacier is to make sure they have adequate rescue gear. This gear should be evenly distributed among the party and readily accessible. Use of rescue gear will be discussed in the next chapter, but in general it should consist of prusiks tied on the rope ahead of each climber, pulleys, both long and short runners and/or cordelettes, anchors appropriate to the surface conditions, belay devices, and spare carabiners. Following this system, a party of three on a temperate glacier is minimally but adequately equipped for a crevasse rescue if each member clips on a pulley, a runner, an anchor, and two or three spare carabiners, as well as their prusiks or ascenders. Ice axes in hand, the team is ready to embark, assuming that they know where they're going.

ROUTEFINDING

When you look up at a glaciated mountain from below you usually can't see many of the crevasses, so when you follow your planned route you'll probably come across some gaping surprises. If you can somehow get an overview of your glacier, a much more reliable route can be plotted. From an overlooking hill you can often see the patterns and concentrations of the glacier's crevasses and icefalls, as well as avalanche and serac fall zones. Aerial photos can provide the best view, and an airplane's perspective is the only high one available on big glaciers like those in Alaska and the Yukon.

Once you're underway on a route, glacier terrain can look much different than it did from far away, and you may be tempted to alter your original plans. But unless you come across barriers or options that you couldn't have seen from afar, weigh heavily the wisdom of your overview.

Whether you can get an overview or not, the basic principle of routefinding is to look for the smoothest, most direct terrain to get you where you want to go. A wrinkled, broken surface will hold more crevasses and take more care to get through. The important thing is to plan the entire route as much as possible. Plot how one section should lead to the next, and the next after that, to avoid sending yourself toward a dead end. Usually there are trade-offs—going over some rougher terrain here to avoid a big 'schrund there. Whatever scoping you do will pay off, but rarely can a route be plotted with complete certainty. It's not unusual to find a huge maw where you thought there would be easy cruising, but this is what adventure is all about, no?

Keeping track of your progress on a map can pay off if you come across features that cause you to change course, or if clouds come in and cause a whiteout.

In the winter and early spring, when snow smoothes the terrain, one can't always be sure where the simple mountain slopes end and

*"In making those trips over the glaciers when I passed over a crevasse
I stepped pretty light. At such times I don't believe I weighed an ounce."*

—Tom Lloyd during (unroped) first
ascent of Mount McKinley, 1910. From
The Sourdough Expedition. Terrence Cole.

the crevassed glacier begins. In this case, "outside" information can be
the best guide, especially previous experience in the area, a good topographical map (although many glaciers have advanced or retreated dra-
matically since most maps were compiled), or aerial photos. Also, the
lower reaches of sizable glaciers are generally confined to valleys, while
almost all slopes in the upper reaches of a glacier's basin will be glaciated,
crevassed terrain. When there's doubt, treat it as crevasse country
and rope up.

THE ROPE LEADER

While overall route planning usually comes out of a team discussion,
the rope leader, by virtue of his or her position at the front of the party,
must discover the route's details. It's he or she who decides whether to
go around crevasses or over them, when to fan out *en echelon* (described
later in this chapter), and whether or not a place is likely to be safe for
gathering together.

Depending on the glacier and its condition, the rope leader's job
can be casual or harrowing. The leader needs to start assessing the likelihood of crevasse falls before even getting on the glacier. Once underway,
the leader continually evaluates the strength and predictability of the
snow, taking the team either over or around snowbridges. A wise leader
will take a very conservative approach at first, at least until more information has been gathered along the way. If conditions are obviously solid,
the leader will soon be walking or hopping across the smaller crevasses
without breaking stride. If conditions are obviously hazardous, the leader
will poke around and weave a course as if through a minefield.

The rope leader tries to balance two somewhat contradictory
demands: safety and speed. No one wants to walk into a crevasse, but
no one wants to spend a whole morning getting around one either.
The rope leader decides whether a faster, more direct route (generally

◄ *David Wilson rappelling over a bergschrund on the west face of Yerupajá, Peru* speaking, a route crossing a crevasse) offers enough safety compared to a longer, apparently less dangerous route (generally a route circumventing a crevasse).

It might be easy for the safety-conscious to say, "Always take the longer, safer route," but in many cases speed is safety, especially when conditions will deteriorate with time—as they often do. The sun of a hot day melting snowbridges, a storm or whiteout, nightfall moving in (whether imminently or eventually), avalanche or icefall hazards from above—all of these are hazards that a team can best deal with by just plain moving fast. Detours can further exact a cost in the members' fatigue level, slowing travel even more. On the other hand, one should not risk, say, a fifty-fifty chance of taking a crevasse plunge if it can be avoided in any way, for a crevasse fall can demand all the time, energy, and stress a team can spare.

When rope leaders encounter a suspected or obvious snowbridge, they can probe its depth and width with an ice ax. A long ice ax with a smooth shaft can be helpful here; a ski pole with a small basket is even better. When a probe finds less resistance, beware! If there's no better alternative bridge or end run, crossing the fragile bridge can be safer on hands and knees, or even lying prone, to spread body weight over a greater surface area. If a crevasse's walls are obviously solid and not too far apart, it may be possible to leap over the gap, although great leaps are less commonly possible than photographers would have us believe.

SURVIVAL INSTINCTS

After a number of years of climbing, I landed a job as a guide and instructor for the North Cascades Alpine School. There, more than anywhere else in the Lower 48, glacier travel and crevasse rescue were primary concerns of everyday life. We guides discussed and debated all the subtleties we came across, from harness design to hauling ratchets. We held to strict standards for traveling with clients; it pained us to see other parties who apparently saw no need for a rope or who tied into swami belts without leg loops. Very few teams traveled with anchors or pulleys handy. We shared stories such as the couple walking hand-in-hand down the glacier, the rope dragging behind in a long picturesque loop. We knew that sooner or later we'd be rescuers.

Descending Mount Baker one afternoon, my party crossed a particularly tenuous snowbridge, and the last guy in our team of three broke through it. His fall didn't pull hard on the rope, but he was hidden below the surface. I instructed the adjacent guy to hold firm while I checked the situation. Another guy happened to be coming by on his way up to camp. He was shirtless and unroped, but had a rope strapped onto his full pack.

I saw my client stuck half into the deteriorating snowbridge over a very black abyss, held in an awkward position he couldn't wrench out of. The shirtless guy reached down to pull him out, and I yelled for him to get away. He responded that he had the situation under control. I scurried to set an anchor while he jumped over the crevasse and took off his pack to better help the stuck man. I dug in a fluke as fast as I could, and while "Shirtless" was on his knees tugging at the client's arm, I put a C-pulley rig onto the rope. Shirtless and I yelled back and forth some more about who had the situation under control. About the time he was bracing in a new position to yank from, I had the pulley rigged, and I heaved the client up so he could wrestle to his feet.

Shirtless waved good-bye and resumed his hike up to his campsite. We waved back, figuring that anyone who'd survived to a majority age with so little common sense probably had gifts beyond our capacities.

TEAM TRAVEL

When a team travels roped together, how the members manage their progress affects their well-being in two important ways. First, how the rope runs at the time of a crevasse fall has a great effect on how serious the crevasse fall will be. Second, the amount of consideration and team-work each member practices can greatly affect partnerships—and, for instance, whether or not he or she will have tent space to share that night.

To minimize the seriousness of crevasse falls, the most important thing team members can do is to keep as much slack as possible out of the rope between them. Any slack in the rope is distance that a falling climber accelerates (at 32 feet per second!) *before* the adjacent partner can begin to brake the fall. With a slack-free rope, the force comes onto the adjacent partner immediately, before the falling climber gets very far into the hole and before the fall generates an impact velocity. Thus, with a slack-free rope most crevasse falls can be held simply by leaning against the pull (see fig. 2.5), without resorting to ice-ax arrest.

Slack-free does not mean taut, however. Ideally, the rope simply drapes from each climber's harness and runs to the next with neither slack nor tension (see fig. 2.6). A climber who constantly pulls rope tension on his partners generates emotional tension as well.

Glacier travel would be a simple matter of parading together on a snug rope if it weren't for people's different paces, and for hills and corners in the way. These factors must be coordinated. Obviously, the team can go no faster than its slowest member; faster climbers must have patience, and dawdling climbers must consider their partners! Other than this, a simple rule of thumb can greatly help rope coordination: each member tries to keep the proper amount of slack in the rope ahead.

By this rule, when one member starts up a hill and slows down, the partner behind slows down as well. When the person ahead reaches easier ground or starts downhill, the partner behind tries to speed up, although the person ahead must also take it a bit easier. Experienced travelers can anticipate speeding and slowing, and at appropriate times give bursts of effort to steady the overall progress, knowing that a slowing rest will come shortly.

In addition to keeping the rope free of slack, to reduce the seriousness of crevasse falls members need to be concerned with keeping the rope perpendicular to the direction of the surrounding crevasses. When a climber falls into a crevasse and the rope is oblique to the crevasse wall,

Figure 2.5   Holding a moderate crevasse fall

he or she will pendulum farther into it (accelerating at something less than 32 feet per second), coming to rest at a point directly below the adjacent partner who held the fall. With the rope nearly *paralleling* a crevasse there's also the danger that two or more members will end up over the same crevasse, and if one goes in the other(s) probably will too.

Thus, when a rope leader chooses to circumvent a crevasse, the other members heading around it should not follow the leader's tracks to the edge of the crevasse; they should start moving in the leader's direction, keeping the rope as perpendicular to the crevasse as possible. Of course, they also must be careful not to walk into another crevasse.

Turning a corner, which usually means end-running a crevasse, requires similar but more subtle coordination (see fig. 2.7). As the forward member starts around the corner, the following member still travels

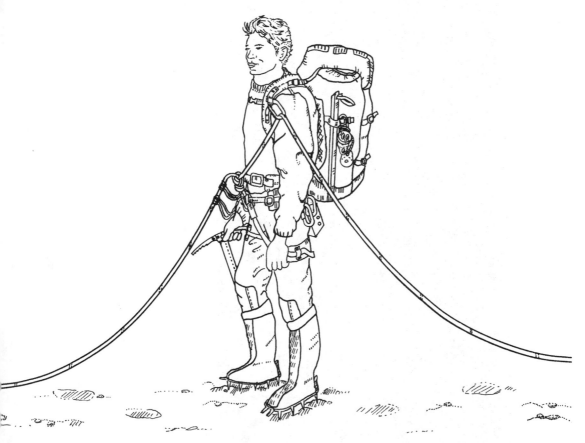

Figure 2.6   Appropriate amount of slack rope

"Among glacier ambuscades a party that has not found unity will fall to pieces."

—Geoffrey Winthrop Young,
1946. *Mountaincraft.*

somewhat toward the other, and slack tends to accumulate (see figs. 2.7a and 2.7b). Thus the lead member should speed up some and the following one should slow (see fig. 2.7c). When the rope span is halfway "around" the corner they reach an inflection point, and the two travel somewhat away from each other, tending to generate tension. To compensate, the lead member slows and the following one speeds up (see fig. 2.7d).

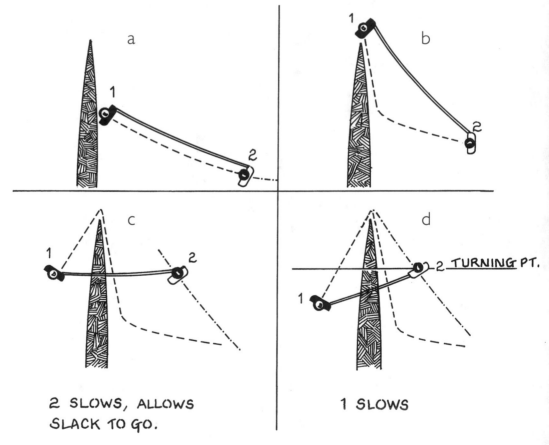

Figure 2.7 *Turning a corner or end-running a crevasse (top view)*

When crevasses run generally perpendicular to a team's intended route, keeping the rope perpendicular to them poses little problem. But when the crevasses generally parallel a route, the only solution is to travel **en echelon**, where members travel not in the leader's path, but take their own parallel course off to the side (see fig. 2.8). While *en echelon*, team members ideally travel in the same direction, but on opposite sides of the crevasses. All members must coordinate their individual courses with their partners.

Ideal conditions for traveling *en echelon* don't arise often, however. Crevasse systems can lead members in different directions, making it difficult to coordinate travel or even to return together. In a heavily crevassed area one member might come to a dead end and then the whole team must retreat until that member can find a way around. Too, if there are novices in the party it might be wise to not trust their ability to avoid crevasses on their own. This means that, before deciding to fan out, a party must balance potential safety with practicality.

WHITEOUTS

Glaciers exist because they're in cloudy places that receive more snow than sunshine, and it's an unfortunate fact that light refracts through clouds about the same way it reflects off snow—giving clouds and snow the same white color. All too often clouds envelop a glacier, making the world white, destroying any sense of depth, diffusing even the nearest bumps and dips into a seemingly infinite, omnipotent whiteness. Disorientation in such a featureless world can be profound even in a familiar

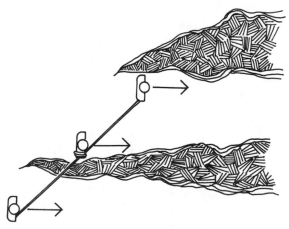

Figure 2.8 Traveling en echelon

area, and it can seep into the emotional corners of the mind. Even experienced climbers have made the most basic mistakes in whiteouts, for example mistaking east for west while looking at their compasses. So, the first rule about traveling in whiteouts is don't.

When the first rule must be broken, the second rule is to assess the situation analytically, gathering all the information available to you. It's very helpful to have your own or someone else's tracks definitely leading where you want to go, but realize how dependent you are on those tracks. Think twice about going farther if there's a chance of snowfall or wind filling them in. When snowfall is likely to obscure crucial tracks, climbers will mark their routes with wands, as close as a rope's length apart if conditions have the potential to get really bad. A trick for introducing some contour to the ground immediately in front of you is to toss snowballs ahead; with this added texture you can at least see what angle the nearby ground runs at. If it gets to this point though, your best hope may be clever use of map and compass.

For a map to help, you need to establish where you are on the map, and plot a course on it to where you want to go. You'll need to locate yourself as precisely as possible, potentially with only one piece of information: the direction of up and down. Take a compass bearing directly down your whited-out slope, and on the topographical map find the slopes on which you could possibly be standing—that is, slopes where the contour lines run perpendicular to your reading (see fig. 2.9). Chances are there won't be more than a couple of possible slopes. To help you find just where you are on that slope, an altimeter can be

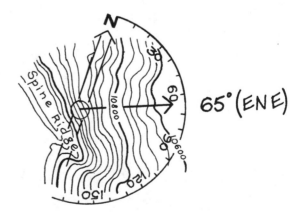

65° (ENE)

Figure 2.9 Compass bearing directly downslope will be perpendicular to contour lines on map

invaluable. Of the altimeters commonly available, only the expensive ones are accurate enough to be really helpful, and even these should be calibrated to a mapped elevation at least once a day.

Once you've formed a hypothesis of where you are, plot a course on the map, and take careful note of the aspects of the slopes that your planned route should cross. Then set your compass to the bearing of your plotted route and start out on that bearing. As you go, frequently compare the aspects of the slopes you've traveled (by taking bearings directly downhill again) against those of your hypothesized plot. Based on this, you can reevaluate your hypothesis and, if the new information doesn't jibe, make a new hypothesis.

In following a compass bearing, it can help to give the compass to the person behind the lead member. This second person sights along the rope going to the leader and directs the course; the lead member has nothing to sight against, and will more easily stray from the bearing. The best attitude for successful whiteout travel is to find and trust the compass readings with mathematical fervor. The one who gets lost in the fog often is the one who decides that intuition is smarter than the needle. Many who plan extensive icefield trips use Global Positioning System devices.

These procedures can work easily in an area with relatively "typical" slopes, but in gentle, featureless terrain or heavily crevassed, "densely featured" terrain they can present serious challenges. The record includes both successes and failures. One party traversing an icefield in the Canadian Coast mountains followed careful compass readings through a complete whiteout for 20 miles, and found a crucial cache. On the other hand, an experienced friend of mine chose to wait out a whiteout storm on the Columbia Icefield. After two failed attempts to exit, and with no food or fuel left, he and his partner dug a cave and waited five days before visibility returned.

HOLDING FALLS: THE GLACIER TRAVELER'S BELAYS

Usually team members depend on one another's body weight, readiness, and ability to ice-ax arrest (in that order) to hold their crevasse falls. Warnings from the leader about potentially weak bridges can serve to remind team members about the importance of maintaining a slack-free rope, since the force of a crevasse fall bearing on a partner via a snug rope often won't pull the partner off balance. If it does, then he or she immediately goes into ice-ax arrest. In areas that are potentially more dangerous, it's smart to carry your ax in an ice-ax arrest grip.

A problem with depending on an ice-ax arrest is the inherent droop of slack rope when members travel together—slack that allows acceleration in a fall. Therefore, hazardous crevasse crossings call for a more substantial belay, where the adjacent partner eliminates all slack and focuses on holding a potential fall. There are four general cases when a belay might be needed (see fig. 2.10):

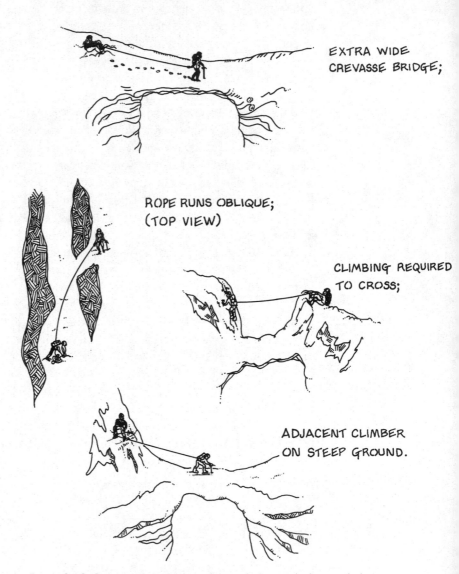

EXTRA WIDE CREVASSE BRIDGE;

ROPE RUNS OBLIQUE; (TOP VIEW)

CLIMBING REQUIRED TO CROSS;

ADJACENT CLIMBER ON STEEP GROUND.

Figure 2.10 Dangerous situations where a belay might be needed

1. Crossing fragile bridges over wide crevasses.
2. Crossing fragile bridges where for one reason or another the rope runs oblique to the crevasse.
3. Crevasse crossings where one must climb down the near wall and/ or climb out the opposite wall.
4. When the adjacent climber is on steep and/or icy ground above the crevasse.

Of course, what is "wide," "oblique," or "steep" is a matter of judgment. Also, in any of these situations, the severity of the force on the adjacent or belaying climber will be much greater if the crevasse lip is hard and icy.

For places where the potential fall does not justify the set-up time of a full anchored-belay, the **boot-ax belay** is the most common quick belay. Operated properly, a boot-ax belay should offer improved security over arrest readiness, as the belayer carefully monitors the rope to keep out all slack. Yet with practice it takes but seconds to set up. It should only be used when another ropemate is ready to back up the belayer and to come anchor the rope for rescue if necessary.

Carefully study the drawing of the boot-ax belay (see figs. 2.11a to 2.11d). This is how to set it up:

1. Sink your ax nearly to the head, tilting it away from the potential force about 45 degrees. You might have to stamp on it to get it into hard, late-summer snow, or in soft conditions you might have to stamp down a firmer platform.

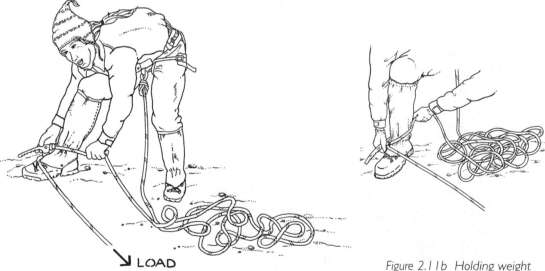

↘ LOAD

Figure 2.11a Boot-ax belay

Figure 2.11b Holding weight
with a boot-ax belay

2. Loop the rope around the shaft (see fig 2.11b).
3. Press your "uphill" boot—the one away from the load—against the shaft under both strands of file rope, and take the rope in your "downhill" hand (see fig. 2.11c). This is your brake hand, ready to hold a fall by wrapping the rope around your ankle, thereby bending the rope in an S curve. Take careful note of the solid stance shown, with the climber ready to lean on the bent "uphill" leg (fig. 2.11a).

To hold a fairly hard fall with this belay, you must be practiced and ready to make it a dynamic belay. That is, you must dissipate the force of the fall gradually, by letting rope through for a second or two, wrapping it around your ankle gradually. The boot-ax belay cannot be expected to hold a hard fall statically without any rope paying out—the ax and your stance will rip out.

A practiced belayer can set up a boot-ax belay literally in seconds, and with reasonably good snow and a solid, balanced stance it can hold a surprising force. However, as with any belay designed to hold only moderate falls, it is imperative to practice and develop judgment about when it can and cannot be trusted. Spend time with a partner on a steep slope of summer snow, taking in and paying out rope, and practicing mock falls with it.

When you're faced with the relatively unusual case of a fairly serious crevasse crossing, you'll want to set up an **anchored-sitting belay**, just as in rock or ice climbing (see fig. 2.12). It will take more time to set an anchor and rig this belay, but with a well-placed anchor in reasonable

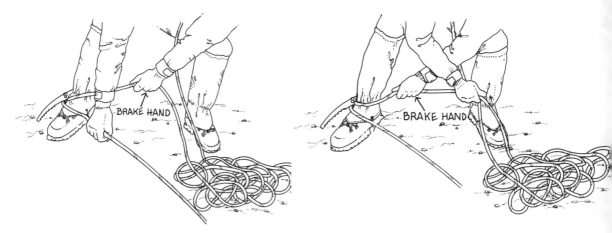

Figure 2.11c Paying out rope   Figure 2.11d Taking in rope

ANCHOR

Figure 2.12 Anchored-sitting belay

snow it will hold the force of virtually any crevasse fall. Anchors are discussed in the chapter on rescues, so at this point suffice it to say that when you set an anchor, make sure you set it to hold in the direction that the potential fall will come from. Tie into the anchor with a runner or the climbing rope, sit down between the climber and the anchor with a minimum of slack in your tie-in, and rig a hip belay or belay device. Compared to a hip belay, a belay device is more foolproof, and is easily rigged with a pack on. It's a good idea to carry a belay device for use in a rescue-hauling rig anyway, as described in the rescue chapter.

When setting up any belay across a crevasse, it's crucial to realize that if a climber does fall very far at all, the rope will have to be anchored off. With three or more in a party this usually isn't a problem, as a free member should be able to come over to the belay and do the job. But a two-person party must take this fact more seriously, as the belayer will have to anchor the rope alone, while holding the weight of the fallen partner.

ICE SLOPES

Many crevasse injuries and fatalities are the result of falls from icy slopes, where a waiting crevasse was a catchment. There are two primary concerns here. First, icy slopes demand critical climbing skill, with crampons absolutely fixed to your boots, sure posture over your crampons, and positive use of your ice ax. The unforgiving consequences of a fall insist that relaxed concentration and accurate footwork be maintained all the time.

Second, glacier travelers on an icy slope need to recognize when they cannot depend on ice-ax arrest to stop a fall. Too often, teams roped together for crevasses progress up onto an icy slope where an unanchored rope only ensures that one falling climber will pull off other teammates. It's critical to recognize and prepare for this transition from a snowbridge hazard to a slope hazard. Ice-ax arrest can be counted on to stop falls on moderate slopes with favorable snow conditions, but few people fall on this type of ground. Steeper, icier slopes where falls are more likely require additional backup.

The **running belay** (or **simul-climb**) system is a way to keep moving efficiently on moderate slopes where a backup is wanted. The leader drills in an ice screw or drives in a picket, and clips the running rope to it. The team then keeps moving together, with the following members adjusting their pace to keep out extra slack. If the going is easy and the anchors are solid, the leader may choose to have only one anchor along the rope's length, or if the team is challenged or the anchors are dubious, as many new anchors as deemed necessary can be set and clipped. When rope partners reach an anchor they clip past it, and the last member to reach it notifies the leader. If it hasn't been done already, the leader adds a new anchor while the last member collects the old one.

Regardless of the belay system, a team is inherently safer traveling diagonally on a slope instead of directly up or down, because any fall in that scenario will be a pendulum, bringing the force onto teammates and anchors slowly instead of at the sharp end of a plummet. If the slope is icy and/or so steep that any members in the party are reaching the limit of their climbing ability, the team should initiate an anchored belayer-leader system.

AVALANCHES

Winter persists for a majority of the year in glacial terrain, and winter mountaineers who want to live long lives look out for avalanche conditions and avalanche-prone slopes. Avalanches occur when bonds in the snowpack fail; therefore, some of the conditions that cause weak snowbridges can also cause avalanches. For instance, a substantial spring or summer storm followed by a warm sunny day will generate mushy bridges and probably wet snow avalanches as well.

Most avalanches on glacial terrain come during or soon after heavy storms, or when daytime melting is especially strong. Slopes of 30 to 45 degrees—moderate steepness—stand at a middle angle that's shallow enough to accumulate deposits, but steep enough to release an unstable slab. It's smart to stay away from these slopes for at least one day following a big snowstorm. This gives the new snow a chance to settle, and the climbing party a chance to assess the hazard. With time most slopes either strengthen or avalanche, although instability can persist for weeks in cold regions. Avalanche prediction blends refined science with experienced guesswork, and all alpine travelers should get training in it.

SERAC FALL

Wherever a glacier pours over a steep area the ice breaks into walls and seracs that periodically tumble. These ice avalanches are mountaineering's most awesome hazard. Expeditions spend considerable time assessing the relative danger of different areas of serac fall, then taking careful steps to minimize exposure time in the danger zones.

If avalanche study mixes some guesswork with refined science, then predicting serac fall mixes precious little science with a world of guesswork. In this game there is only one certainty: walls that have released blocks in the past will do so again. The pertinent questions are, how often does a given wall release, and what area will be hit?

When assessing the hazard to a certain area, know that if seracs look unstable and tottering, they are. Ice walls that have scalloped, fresh facets have unleashed a cataclysm recently, and you can probably see the crumbled fragments on the ground below. Look carefully (from a distance!) at the amount, scale, scope, and freshness of this debris. Sometimes these fragments are lightly buried under new snowfall, and show as "tombstone" lumps on a debris cone. On an expedition, try to watch the area for many days while you get used to the altitude and plan your trip. In any case, make a guess as to whether the walls in question calve daily, weekly, monthly, annually, or hourly. Then compare your estimation of calving frequency with the time you expect to spend on a possible route in the danger zone. Usually, each serac area has active spots that release repeatedly for awhile. Places that are obviously suicidal as well as places with minimal serac hazards are easy to figure. It's the seracs that only go occasionally that make for tough decisions.

Climbers have spent countless hours pondering how much melting daytime temperatures help trigger serac fall. It certainly seems as if serac

fall activity goes up during the day, but every mountaineer has heard the sound of icefall from a sleeping bag. Teams that must weave through serious icefalls, such as south-side routes to Mount Everest, often set a noon deadline to be out of the danger zone. Some experienced climbers say that serac fall increases at the warmest part of the day, and also at the coldest wee hours. This may be because very cold ice is more brittle and therefore weak. Heavy snowfall puts added weight on seracs, which also increases their likelihood of calving. Finally, anecdotal evidence suggests that seasons following especially heavy winters may have a higher rate of serac fall.

Although we ponder much to distinguish relative safety from relative hazard, smart decisions are based on the knowledge that the constant of gravity is the primary force behind serac falls, and so the only sure way to reduce the chance of getting hit by serac fall is to spend less time under serac walls. Certainly climbers should avoid placing camps or taking rest stops in hazardous areas. Even under relatively safe seracs, if there is a safer spot nearby, stack the odds in your favor and keep going to the safest spot around before stopping.

GATHERING TOGETHER

Most rest stops can be taken with the members still stretched apart along their rope, but when a team does gather together and slacken the rope, the lead member and the party as a whole must choose the spot carefully. To make sure the area hides no crevasses, the leader should probe it with the rope still stretched out. Then the last member into the site should be brought in with a boot-ax belay, and the established "safe zone" should be made known to all members, perhaps with wands. When leaving the spot the rope leader should then receive a belay. Any time a party stays in one place, they of course should be especially careful to be out of the way of icefall, rockfall, or avalanche runout.

TRAVEL ON A "DRY" ABLATION ZONE

Where no snow covers a glacier's ice skeleton, travel precautions are much different. There are no snowbridges to break through and all the crevasses are apparent. But to simply travel roped up as on a snowy surface is to court disaster; members cannot hold falls on the ice, and a rope merely assures that one person's fall will include the rest. Hence,

◀ *David Wilson exiting the Yerupajá Glacier, Cordillera Huayhaush, Peru* members travel unroped as they would on rock or general alpine terrain, unless the climbing is steep and/or exposed enough to require an anchored belay.

CAMPING CONSIDERATIONS

Disposal of human waste is a serious concern on a glacier, and there is no ideal answer. The first choice is to defecate off the glacier, in soil or moraine where water contamination is minimized. If you must go on the glacier, get the waste into a deep crevasse. Usually in camp this means you dig a potty and line it with a bag stretched out between wands for later transport to a crevasse. Bags should be either biodegradable plastic or (in fair weather) paper grocery sacks, doubled in either case.

Another possibility on a temperate glacier in the summer is to camp near a crevasse with a solid edge, making this a direct latrine. Set an anchor and fix a rope to the edge, making sure that there's no overhanging lip (or else clearing a small lip away), and with a swami tie-in and prusik self-belay members can lean back and, well, unload. Direct crevasse latrines are certainly preferred while on the go, and for this reason it's better to have a harness with leg loops that drop away, or else you'll have to rig a separate waist belt.

Camping near a solid crevasse also allows sound disposal of urine and food waste. If a solid-edged crevasse is unavailable, a urination site should be designated so the waste will be concentrated. Remember that on a glacier the water source is the snow.

We can only speculate if crevasse-buried waste does or does not contaminate glacial melt-water; certainly much depends on the type of glacier and the distance from the terminus. But crevasse burial is certainly better than surface burial, which melts out.

Some land managers now require that all fecal waste be carried out. Kayakers' dry-bag technology can help make this a simple, hygienic operation. All litter should be carried out, just as in any backcountry area.

A couple of final aesthetic courtesies: camp at least a short distance off a well-traveled trail so other climbers don't have to walk through your campsite; and retrieve and pack out any wands you've placed.

CHAPTER 3
RESCUE TECHNIQUES FOR THE GLACIER TRAVELER

The previous chapter discussed the precautions that glacier travelers can take to guard against crevasse falls. But being prepared and careful doesn't change the fact that an occasional fall into a crevasse is a part of traveling on glaciers. Therefore, knowing how to ascend out of a crevasse and how to haul a partner out of one have long been acknowledged as essential skills for the glacier traveler. This chapter outlines the fundamentals of these skills, and the following chapter adds more advanced techniques to make crevasse rescue reliable in more situations.

ASCENDING SYSTEMS

Most crevasses trap victims between unclimbable walls of soft snow overhung by looser snow. So to get out of a typical crevasse a person needs to have a system for ascending the rope. Big-wall climbers, spelunkers, and glacier travelers all have developed various systems for ascending a rope. Each system uses a set of two or more rope-gripping devices, either mechanical ascenders or prusik (or similar) knots. With all your weight on one ascender or knot, the other, unweighted one can be moved up the rope; then you shift all your weight to the "new" one and raise the other, repeating the process up the rope. As well as using various knots or camming devices, systems differ in how they connect body parts to the knots or ascenders.

The **prusik knot** has served as a tried-and-true rope-gripping device for decades now, and all glacier travelers should be practiced with it. The **Bachman variation** (see Appendix 2) is favored by many for ease of movement. Tiny mechanical devices offer even greater conve-

◀ *Greg Collum working through a moat/crevasse complex on the Tiedemann Glacier, British Columbia Coast Mountains*

nience and easier operation than knots. Full-size, "big-wall" ascenders are also faster and easier to use than knots, but few glacier travelers justify their weight and expense unless they need them anyway for their climbing objective. Some do not grip well on icy ropes. With any mechanical ascending device, one must be careful to not install it where it might receive a shock load, as this can damage the rope.

A prusik knot is made from a loop of supple rope, usually 6-millimeter perlon. The best knot to tie the loop is a grapevine or "double fisherman's" knot. To make a prusik knot from the loop you simply wrap it through itself two or three times around a rope of larger diameter (see fig. 3.1). Essentially, then, the prusik knot is a double or triple girth hitch. Straighten the wraps so that they coil cleanly and snugly around the main rope. The wraps grab when you pull on the open loop, the more you pull the more tightly they grab, because the wraps are snugging onto themselves. But when you loosen the wraps and hold them directly, they slide freely along the main rope. After a person's body weight has wrenched the wraps tightly, an easy way to loosen them is to press against the single "opposing" wrap designated in the drawing.

A prusik's friction relies on the suppleness and smaller diameter of the prusik cord. With climbing ropes of either 9 or 11 millimeters in diameter, the best compromise between strength and bite is a 6-millimeter prusik. However, a somewhat stiff 6-millimeter prusik on a somewhat stiff 9-millimeter rope will definitely need that third wrap to keep it from slipping. When new, a single strand of 6-millimeter perlon rope will hold up to 1,700 pounds, but it should nevertheless be replaced frequently. Some climbers favor marine-braid Dacron cord for their prusiks because its very supple sheath grabs extremely well. However, be aware that this softer sheath wears faster than the stiffer but tougher perlon. The new 5.5-millimeter, soft-weave Spectra cord seems to be a

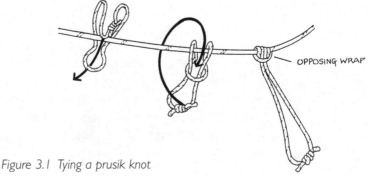

Figure 3.1 Tying a prusik knot

suitable ultra-strong prusik material. Kevlar cord should never be used for a prusik because it's quite stiff and its fibers readily break down with repeated flexing.

Of all the connecting systems, the **Texas system** has drawn the most favor among glacier travelers for its simplicity, lightness, comfort, and ease of use. It consists of a simple prusik loop (made from 40 to 45 inches of cord) clipped to a locking or doubled carabiner on the seat harness, plus a second prusik knot with a pair of extensions and small loops for the feet (see fig. 3.2).

The foot loops, or "stirrups," are best constructed from a single strand 10 to 12 feet long, as follows:

1. In the middle of this strand tie a figure eight with a bight at least 6 inches long.
2. Stand and hold this bight at your diaphragm with the two strands draped down to the ground.
3. At the point where each strand reaches the ground, tie an overhand knot that leaves a bight of about 3 inches. Test your system, and trim off any extra cord.

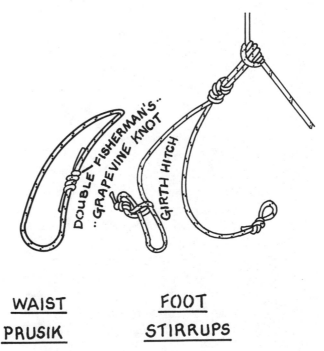

WAIST
PRUSIK

FOOT
STIRRUPS

Figure 3.2 Texas prusik system

To make these overhand knots into a cinching loop for a boot of any size, with or without crampons, you simply feed the main cord through the loop as a girth hitch.

When roping up for glacier travel, wrap both the waist and stirrup prusiks on the rope between you and a partner, the stirrups adjacent to your harness, the waist loop next to them. Clip the waist prusik to a locking carabiner on the harness, and either tuck the stirrups away in a pocket, or knot and clip them off on the harness. If you're using palm-size mechanical ascenders, you can travel with them on the rope also. In either case, make sure that the prusik or ascender connection to your harness has slack, or else it will take the force of a fall. This can damage the prusik, or the ascender can damage the rope. If you're using big-wall ascenders, keep them handy on the harness, *not* on the rope, because in a crevasse fall the weighty objects spring up at about face level and typically knock the victim silly. Most models can readily be put on the rope when needed.

Here's a summary of how to ascend with the Texas system (see fig. 3.3a to c):

1. Girth-hitch your feet into the stirrups, then stand tall in them. To keep strain off your arms while standing up, bring your feet under your buttocks and press up using your thighs (see fig. 3.3a).
2. As you rise, loosen the waist prusik and slide it up the rope with you (see fig. 3.3b).
3. Sit back on the waist prusik and lift your feet as high as possible (see fig. 3.3c).
4. With the weight now off the stirrups, slide them up as high as possible, even to where they meet the waist prusik.
5. Kick your feet under your buttocks to stand tall and repeat the process.

The Texas system keeps your weight balanced by having you straddle the rope, and you spend over half your ascent time hanging relatively comfortably in your seat harness. Chest harnesses interfere with raising the waist prusik in this system, so they should be unclipped while ascending.

In any ascending system the only safety is the prusik or ascender that connects to your waist harness. As reliable as most systems are, if you're ascending more than just 15 or 20 feet it's wise to back it up by clipping a bighted figure eight from the main rope right below the lower prusik or ascender into another locking carabiner on your harness.

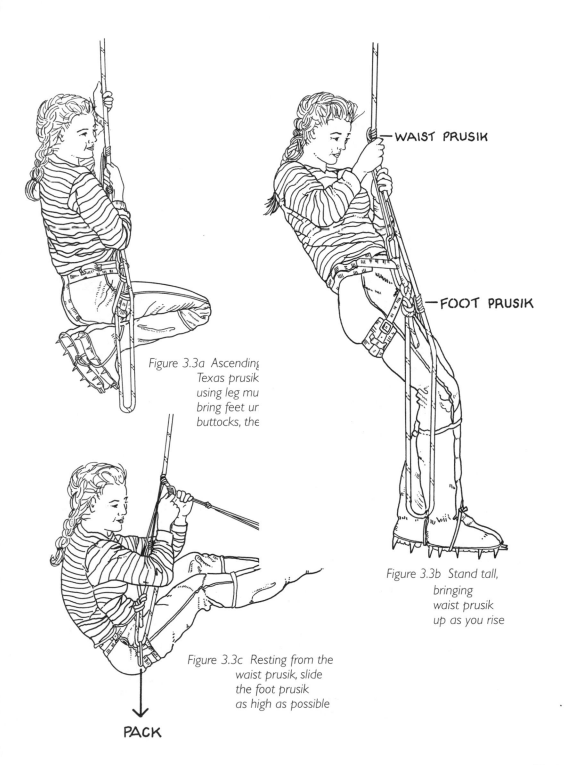

WAIST PRUSIK

FOOT PRUSIK

Figure 3.3a Ascending
Texas prusik
using leg mu
bring feet ur
buttocks, the

Figure 3.3b Stand tall,
bringing
waist prusik
up as you rise

Figure 3.3c Resting from the
waist prusik, slide
the foot prusik
as high as possible

PACK

Whatever ascending system you use, however, it's important to practice using it before it's needed; throwing a rope over a tree limb can make for at least a rudimentary practice session.

PRUSIK OR ASCENDER AS SELF-BELAY

A prusik or ascender can also be used to belay oneself along a rope on a glacier's surface. The prusik or ascender connects from a taut, anchored rope to your seat harness. With full-size ascenders you should clip a carabiner from the bottom of the ascender across the rope; this keeps the ascender in line with the rope. This is advised because when you fall at 90 degrees to the anchor's axis such ascenders tend to lever off the rope. With the prusik or ascender set up, you're free to move along the rope in either direction, sliding the prusik or ascender as you go. Should a snowbridge fail, you must let go of the prusik or ascender and let it hold your fall. As for ascending, it doesn't hurt to back this up with a figure-eight knot clipped into your harness as well. Self-belays come in handy during crevasse rescues; the situations when you're likely to need one are described later.

VICTIM PROCEDURES

One moment you're walking on top of the glacier, the next you're falling, plunging through a chaos of snow and darkness that seems to be dragging you into the bowels of the earth. Then, *boing!* You're jerked to a swinging, sputtering halt, and you look down between cold blue walls into an apparently infinite, dripping blackness.

Your heart races and you strain against a weight still pulling you toward the depths. Oh yes, you recall, the first thing to do after falling in a crevasse is to get your pack off your back, and clip it onto the rope. If you were traveling with the pack already clipped to the rope, you can just heave it off. Eventually you'll want to have it clipped to the rope below your prusiks or ascenders, but for now just get it onto the rope. You can also clip off your ice ax. You may be warm with adrenaline now, but the wet darkness of a crevasse will soon chill you, so next put on some more clothes, especially to keep your hands warm.

Now look around. Is it at all reasonable to walk, climb, or chimney out of the crevasse? Soon one of your buddies will be peering down at you, and a belay or lowering can be arranged. If, however, you can't climb out, and if you actually are dangling in space with your full weight on the rope, there's no reason not to simply start ascending it. True, you don't know what kind of anchor your partners may be fumbling to set up, but with your weight already fully on the rope, unless your ascending system fails there's nothing that ascending can do that they'll even notice. However, if even part of your weight is not on the rope—for example, if you're on a ledge or pressing between crevasse walls don't surprise your partners with any additional load. In this case, wait for someone to peer over and assure you that the rope is well anchored.

Before you start up, clip your pack to the rope below your prusiks or ascenders. This way, as you ascend, the pack's weight will actually help you raise your lower prusik or ascender by keeping tension on the rope, and as you climb the pack will be following you on a two-to-one "pulley." You may have to keep the pack from snagging on small overhangs as you ascend. However, a heavy pack clipped like this will make it difficult or impossible to tie backup knots to your harness, so if the pack is big and your climb out is a long one, have a rope sent down to haul it up.

As you approach the top you'll probably find that the rope disappears into overhanging snow some frustratingly short and desperately steep distance below your goal, the surface. You can shove your prusiks up into the overhang, but to get over the top you'll have to employ any of a few different tricks.

First, you may be able to scoop away much of the overhang with your ax—carefully, though, with upward-directed pushes, because a sharp ice ax can cut a weighted climbing rope as if it were string. Next you'll want to get your prusiks absolutely as far up the rope as possible. Then maybe your buddies can set a prusik above the lip and from it drop down a ladder of runners for you to haul up on. Or you might get enough height if you tie a figure-eight loop in the climbing rope for one foot to stand in; tie this as high as possible right below the lower prusik. With a partner reaching for you with an outstretched ice ax, it usually doesn't take more than a couple of all-out heaves to get you onto the surface.

SURFACE MEMBER PROCEDURES

As mentioned in the introduction, extracting someone from a crevasse can be a fairly technical operation. Before getting into the procedures for surface members it's important to understand two of its primary elements: anchors on a glacier, and the basis of pulley hauling systems.

ANCHORS

As we've said, most crevasse falls occur where a glacier is covered with some sort of soft snow. This is the highly varying medium that glacier travelers usually have to depend on for anchors.

The ubiquitous anchor for snow is the **deadman** or **fluke**, a simple metal plate with attachment cables. It works on the principle that a broad surface buried in the snow will resist a force because to move it you'll have to move all the snow in front of it. Two simple features on a snow fluke increase its reliability many fold. First, a fluke vertically bent so the convex side faces the load will accommodate pulls slightly oblique to the fluke's plane. Second, a fluke's cables should be swaged with the upper cable longer than the lower, so that a simultaneous pull on the two cables leaves the fluke tilted back at 30 to 40 degrees from perpendicular to the pull. With this cant a fluke resists any pressure to rise out of the snow. Set properly, a fluke with these features will actually move through the snow like an airfoil when loaded, deflecting itself down and burying itself deeper. A loop of cord attached to a fluke can make it easier to retrieve once buried (see fig. 3.4).

To place a fluke well, you must first evaluate the snow. In typical old summer snow, you can simply dig the necessary trench (as outlined in this section), but in particularly slushy snow or in never-melted new snow you'll first need to prepare the placement area.

When the snow is quite slushy, you usually just need to scrape away and dig down to the inevitable firmer snow below. But in new, relatively low-density snow, you'll need to simulate age hardening. Essentially this means you dig, overturn and generally upset the snow, then stomp and repack the area. Then, before you dig in to set the fluke, wait five minutes for the broken crystals to rebond into a denser, firmer medium.

One must be wary of placing flukes if there's an icy layer not far under the surface, for such a layer can deflect a fluke upward. The layer can be either an old melt-freeze layer of some sort, or the ice surface of

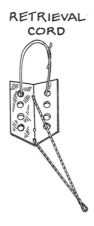

RETRIEVAL CORD

Figure 3.4 Snow fluke

the glacier itself, but in either case you should use another type of anchor.
With the snow ready, you now set your fluke:

1. With the adz of your ax, dig a 1-foot-long trench perpendicular to the load and about a foot deep. Angle this trench about 30 to 40 degrees from perpendicular to the snow surface, the angle of the fluke to its upper cable.

2. With the pick of your ax, slice out a slot from the middle of the trench running toward the load. This slot is for the fluke's cables, and should be as deep as the original trench. This completes a T-shaped site.

3. Stretching the cables toward the load, set the fluke into the trench with the upper cable parallel to the snow surface. Set the fluke into the trench with a combination of pressing down on the fluke and pulling out on the cables.

4. Jerk the cable a couple of times and watch how the fluke reacts. If the fluke rides up when tugged, the cable slot is probably not deep enough, so it's putting a bend in the lower cable that lifts the fluke. Or if the fluke flaps against the trench wall rather than setting deeper, then the trench wall is not canted back enough, or you might have found an icy layer below. If the tugs set the fluke deeper, then you're in business.

In any case, the crustier the snow the more critical it is to set the fluke and its cables at the correct angle. With practice, placing a fluke takes but half a minute or less (see fig. 3.5).

The other well-known snow anchor is the picket, a simple post about 2.5 feet long. Pickets are normally reserved for firmer snow. Other than having a pointed tip for driving into very hard snow and an anchor hole at the top, there are few design considerations in a picket other than surface area.

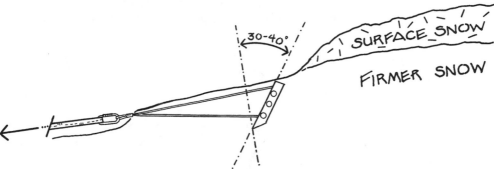

Figure 3.5 Properly placed fluke

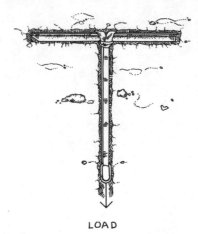

LOAD

Figure 3.6 Picket-deadman anchor

Pickets are simply driven into the snow, and tilted back about 30 degrees from perpendicular to the load. Either hammer blows or boot stamps can pound one into hard snow. Pickets are often the anchor of choice in very firm to hard snow such as old frozen snow or stiff wind-blown snow typical on the higher reaches of mountains. Even in firm conditions, however, it's more likely that a picket will lever out than that a well-placed fluke will fly out.

But there is a method for placing a very reliable picket—bury it sideways as a deadman (see fig. 3.6). As for a fluke, the procedure is as follows:

1. Prepare the snow if necessary, and then dig a trench as long as the picket, about a foot deep and perpendicular to the load. As you dig, undercut the trench toward the load.
2. From the center of the trench dig a trench as deep as the main one but perpendicular to it toward the load. If this trench is not as deep as the original, there will be an upward pull on the picket.
3. Girth-hitch a runner around the center of the picket, and then stamp the picket into the trench with the runner lying in the T trench. Finally, bury and stamp on everything except the tail of the runner.

In most snow conditions you will have a very strong anchor, but you can strengthen it further by plunging a couple of ice axes or pickets

Michael Graber descending toward broken terrain on the west face of Yerupajá, Peru ▶

immediately in front of it. Like any snow or ice anchor, this anchor is directional, only resisting a force perpendicular to the picket. An ice ax with a strong metal or composite shaft works equally well.

ANCHORS IN POOR SNOW CONDITIONS

In extreme conditions, when the snow is deeply slushy (as in low-elevation Alaska in June) or particularly dry (as in the Canadian Rockies in the fall and winter), it may be impossible to set a reliable fluke or picket. One anchor that might work is a couple of plunged ice axes equalized with people leaning on them. Remember, though, that the general theory of snow anchors is to resist a force with surface area. So when the snow is unconsolidated and weak, increase the surface area. For this reason improvised "dead men" can make the strongest anchors—for example, a pack, a pair of skis (ski poles are not strong enough), stuff sacks tightly filled with snow, or a shovel. These can be girth-hitched and thoroughly buried to give the best possible anchor in bad conditions.

ICE SCREWS

When a thin layer of snow covers the icy ablation zone of a glacier, then any crevasse fall will have to be anchored in the ice. The quickest anchor in ice is an ice screw, and in fact an ice screw in solid blue ice is more reliable than any snow anchor. Any of the tubular ice screws available work well in glacier ice, although longer models are much preferred for added strength in the often porous, softer ice of a glacier.

Just as snow anchors depend on snow quality, the most important aspect of a reliable ice screw is the quality of the ice. Glacier ice is wonderfully consistent and not brittle, but usually there's a superficial layer that you'll want to scrape away to get at the solid stuff underneath.

For the relatively moderate but prolonged loads of a rescue, it's crucial to tilt a screw back a bit away from the load—30 to 40 degrees from perpendicular to the load is best. However, the eye of the screw should rest flush against the ice. Here's how to place an ice screw and accommodate both these criteria:

1. Chop a small ledge into the ice at the proper angle for the eye to rest against. By canting your ax pick away from the load at the same angle that the screw will be set in, you can then use the adz to chop exactly the ledge you need in just a few seconds. Often you can just use or enhance a small depression in the ice.
2. Place the screw so that the tip of the eye comes to rest as nearly

as possible at the edge of the ledge, pointing toward the load.

3. When the screw is loaded, the carabiner you clip into the screw should then pull at the desired 30 to 40 degrees from perpendicular to the screw's axis (see fig. 3.7).

It's important to realize that pressure can cause ice to melt, even though the ice temperature remains at or slightly below the freezing point. Thus, during the prolonged loading of a rescue, ice screws can loosen dangerously. For this reason, when rescuing on a summer day with ice-screw anchors it's wise to add a backup anchor, as described farther on in this section. On very warm days ice screws can slowly loosen even without being loaded; to alleviate this you can cover a screw with snow or ice chips and channel away any melt-water running over it.

BOLLARDS

A more tedious but very strong ice anchor is the **bollard**, a teardrop-shaped mushroom chopped out of the ice and looped with rope or webbing. Depending on the density of the ice, a mushroom 2 to 3 feet wide will be plenty strong; in fact, the main risk with a bollard is not the mushroom shearing off, but the rope or webbing rolling off. Therefore, it's the shape of a bollard that makes it safe or unsafe. Make sure that the load pulls downward at least slightly, and that the three sides of the mushroom that will bear the weight are well undercut.

To make a bollard:

1. Look for a relatively high spot where the load will naturally pull downward, then scrape away any superficial snow or ice that won't hold well.

2. Start by chopping the teardrop outline, gradually concentrating more on the three sides that will bear weight. Tubular adzes work best for this.

3. As your groove gets deep, small blows with the ax pick can fine-tune the undercut lip. Before trusting a bollard with someone's weight, loop the rope or webbing over it and see what protrusions if any might lift it off, and eliminate them. A trustworthy bollard distributes the load around a fairly even curve, without the anchor rope running over any high spots (see fig. 3.8).

Even with practice it takes 10 to 20 minutes to chop a good bollard. Though a good one can be stronger than any ice screw and will not melt significantly, because of the time involved most people consider them as a backup to ice screws, or for cases when the need for ice anchors wasn't anticipated and screws are unavailable. One can also make a surprisingly

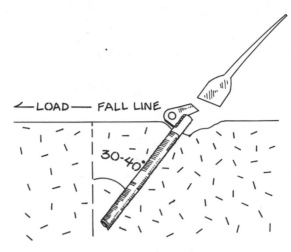

Figure 3.7 Ice screw properly set for rescue anchor; note that the ice-ax head is at the proper angle to chop ledge so that the eye rests flush

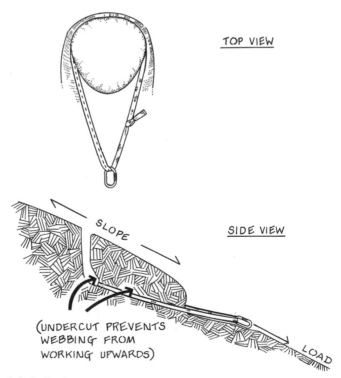

Figure 3.8 Bollard

strong bollard out of firn, although here the mushroom should be at least 6 feet wide and nearly a foot deep.

EQUALIZING AND BACKING UP ANCHORS

Other than a magnificent bollard, no anchor in ice or snow should be solely trusted for a rescue. There are three principal methods for coupling anchors, and which one to use depends on the anchor medium and the gear available.

Backing up. This method involves simply connecting a second anchor to the carabiner of the first one. The connection should have essentially no slack, so that if the first anchor fails or shifts, the weight transfers to the second anchor immediately without generating a shock load.

1. Measure the exact place to set the second anchor by stretching out a runner from the first anchor's carabiner, behind the first anchor.
2. Set the second anchor so that its carabiner reaches just to the end of the new runner (see fig. 3.9a).

This simple system is fine for linking two flukes, because it's normal for the primary fluke to slip a bit once it's loaded, and start sharing the load with the backup.

Tensioned backup. When a primary anchor is already loaded, you can connect the backup with tension so that it shares the load. Do not use this until you are familiar with the tie-off.

1. Set a backup anchor "behind" the first.
2. Run webbing or climbing cord from the carabiner of the backup through a new carabiner on the primary and back toward the backup (see fig. 3.9b).
3. Pull hard on this runner, creating tension between the backup and the load on the primary. Then clip it into the backup's carabiner.
4. While maintaining the tension, tie off the runner with a "slip hitch" tie-off the same as for tying off a belay.

This is an excellent method to reinforce an anchor for hauling, and for linking one equalized pair with a second equalized pair.

Equalizing. Distributing a load between a pair of anchors can more than double the reliability of the overall anchor. Although webbing works fine, this is a good place to use a cordelette, a length (usually 20 to 25 feet) of 6- or 7-millimeter cord (or 5.5-millimeter soft weave Spectra). Many climbers carry a cordelette or two for lots of uses, usually tied in a loop with a double fisherman's knot, then bundled and clipped onto the

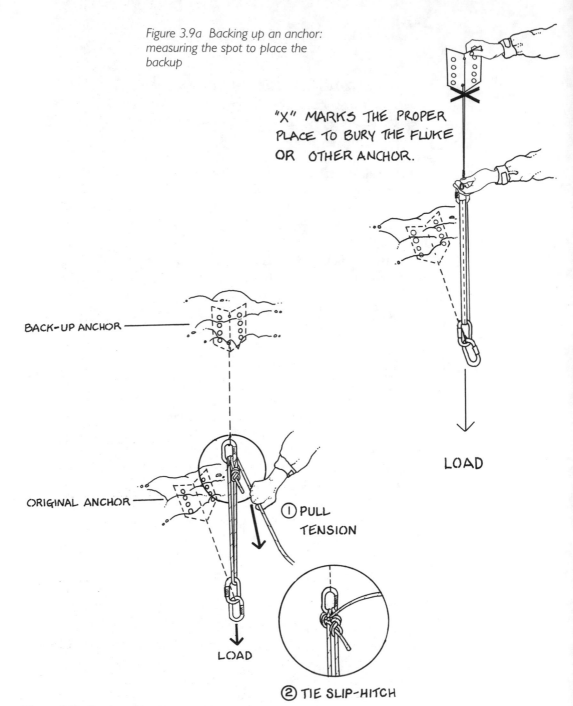

Figure 3.9a Backing up an anchor: measuring the spot to place the backup

"X" MARKS THE PROPER PLACE TO BURY THE FLUKE OR OTHER ANCHOR.

LOAD

BACK-UP ANCHOR

ORIGINAL ANCHOR

① PULL TENSION

LOAD

② TIE SLIP-HITCH

Figure 3.9b Tensioned backup system

harness. Two methods of equalizing anchors are presented here, the first quicker and more widely known, the second safer but slightly more involved.

For the first method:

1. Clip a long runner into both anchors, and make a twist in one of the two strands between them.
2. Clip a third (locking or doubled) carabiner through this twist and across the other strand (see fig. 3.10). When this third carabiner is loaded, the two anchors share the weight between them, even from a range of directions. Should one of the anchors fail the twist will preserve the connection to the other, but the load will come onto the other after some movement, as a potentially severe shock load.

For the second:

1. Clip a cordelette into both anchors (see fig. 3.11).
2. Gather both strands of the cord and pull them directly toward the anticipated load, forming a bight.
3. Tie this bight into an overhand or figure-eight knot. Now you can clip the load to the resulting loop.

If the bight and knot are rigged properly, both anchors share the force equally. What makes this method safer is that if one of the anchors fails, that share of the load comes onto the other anchor immediately, preventing a shock loading. One concern with this system is that if the load

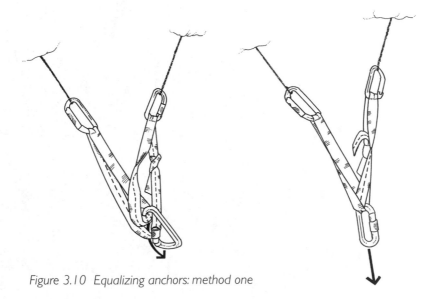

Figure 3.10 Equalizing anchors: method one

changes direction most of the force shifts onto one anchor. But with most rescue loads you should be able to accurately predict the load's direction.

You can also use either method to equalize three or more anchors together. Clip one strand of the cordelette into each anchor, and gather the length between each anchor toward the load. Include the loop between the outermost anchors, and tie the bundle together. To equalize for a range of directions, just twist each strand between anchors into a loop and clip them all into the primary carabiner. You might have to add a runner extension to any distant anchors to have enough cord to equalize more than two anchors.

In any coupling arrangement, the connecting cord or webbing should be long enough to keep the angle between the anchors narrower than 90 degrees. If a short runner connects widely spread anchors, this angle broadens, and a sort of leverage geometrically increases the force on the anchors (see fig. 3.12). If a runner were tightly stretched between

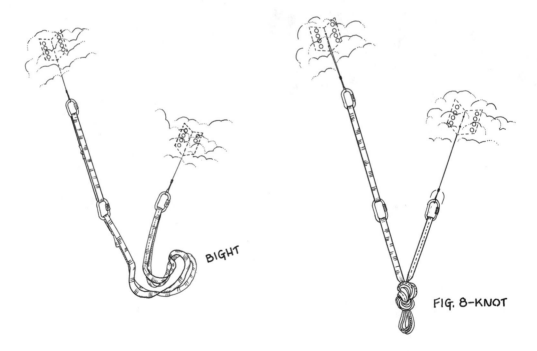

Figure 3.11a Equalizing anchors: method two; clip runners into two anchors

Figure 3.11b Equalizing anchors: method two; tie an overhand or figure-eight knot in a bight

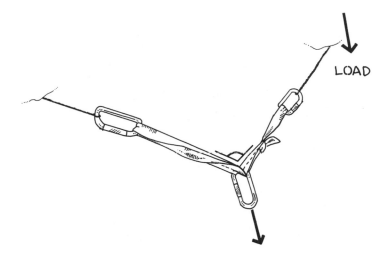

Figure 3.12 Improperly equalized anchors: broad angle multiplies force on anchor

the anchor pair (at 180 degrees from the load), the force theoretically becomes infinite! For this reason anchors should be set slightly behind and slightly apart from one another. Flukes should be set a reasonable distance behind one another, to allow them to move some with added force.

THE ULTIMATE, PREFERRED ANCHOR SYSTEM

The most secure anchor system backs up one equalized anchor pair with another, using four anchors in all. This arrangement is especially recommended for hauling victims using snow anchors. After setting a primary anchor pair, you use one of the backup methods described above —preferably the tensioned backup—to connect the equalizing carabiner of a second pair to the equalizing carabiner of the first.

Because ice and especially snow are such variable mediums, there's no hard and fast rule as to how many anchors are enough for a rescue. In general, trust your intuition: if you're not sure, add more anchors!

THE BASICS OF PULLEY SYSTEMS

It takes a lot of force to haul someone out of a crevasse. Friction of the rope running over the crevasse lip increases the resistance, so that hauling even a partner with no pack generally takes two to five times as much force as a strong climber can generate. Therefore, all but the largest parties have to increase their hauling force by using a pulley system.

In a manner analogous to low gears that enable a bicyclist to climb a hill, pulley systems distribute a load and allow even a single person to haul another out of a crevasse.

The basic **block-and-tackle pulley system** is shown in figure 3.13; the rope is anchored at A, and runs through a pulley, B, which is connected directly to the load. When the end of the rope, C, is pulled, the pulley (and the load as well) moves only half as far as the rope end at C. This means that the work is halved, and the pulley and load receive twice the original force. Another way to look at it is to realize that looping the rope through the pulley back to the anchor generates a second force. This is because the length of rope A-B (between the anchor and the pulley) effectively pulls on the load, too.

This simple system is known as the **C-pulley system**, for the single curve in the rope. Theoretically, it gives a 2-to-1 mechanical advantage, although even with a good rescue pulley that dissipates only 10 percent to friction, the actual multiplying force will be 1.8 to 1. Also, maximum efficiency comes only when the pulling force at C is in line with the pulley and the anchor—that is, when lines A-B and B-C are very close together. For clarity, figure 3.13 has been drawn with the rope coming out

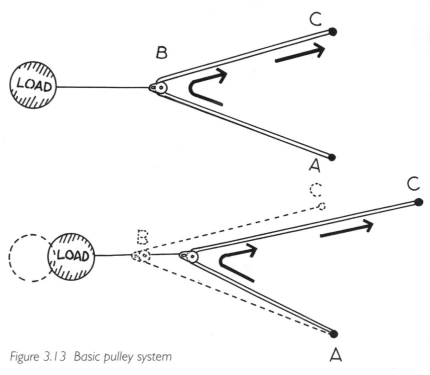

Figure 3.13 Basic pulley system

from the pulley to point C at an angle, but if the force is applied to the side like this, essentially pulling partly away from the system, the force applied at C is less than doubled.

CREVASSE RESCUE PROCEDURES

The general procedures for rescuing a partner from a crevasse are as follows:

1. Stop the fall.
2. Anchor the rope, leaving enough slack to reach the victim.
3. Check the victim, and decide on a rescue method. Generally speaking, the first choice is to have the victim ascend out, as previously described; the second choice is to haul him or her out.
4. Prepare the crevasse lip.
5. Either assist the victim to ascend over the lip, or set up a hauling system.
6. Haul the victim out, if necessary.

With this sequence in mind, we can detail the elements of crevasse rescue.

HOLDING A FALL

Let's return to the well-prepared three-person rope team traveling together on a glacier. Poof! One of the members disappears. The adjacent partner must hold the fall.

As stated previously, if the rope is tight and fairly perpendicular to the crevasse, most snowbridge collapses can be held by simply standing firm and leaning against the pull from the fallen partner. If the rope does not come taut immediately—that is, if the victim is stopped by the snowbridge or narrow walls before the weight of the fall bears onto the partner—the partner should retreat from the crevasse and pull the rope taut. If the force of the fall pulls an adjacent member off his or her feet, then that partner must work into the ice-ax arrest position, as should the next member down the rope. As discussed in chapter 2, the nightmare of being pulled toward an abyss, digging and kicking for every ounce of ice-ax arrest grip, is rare, but it can happen.

Crevasse falls generally end in a split second. In minor "punch-ins" where half the victim's body is still on the surface, then "rescue" is easy. Partners on the surface stand firm with the rope tight, and with this help the victim probably can just struggle out. If the victim is in too far to heave out right away or is stuck, then the surface members should anchor the rope, the first step in a "genuine" rescue.

ANCHORING THE ROPE

Besides keeping the victim from falling any farther, anchoring the rope allows surface members to be belayed out to the crevasse edge to assist or check the victim; it enables the victim to ascend out on the rope, if possible; and it allows the surface members to set up a hauling system.

The first and third criteria make it important to anchor the rope not at its end, but in the midsection, leaving enough slack to reach the victim. This is where the proper spacing of members discussed in chapter 2 becomes critical. Assuming a three-person rope team has an end member fall, here's the procedure for anchoring the rope:

1. The middle member holds the rope taut, either in ice-ax arrest or by leaning against the pull.
2. The free member on the end of the rope comes down to "below" the middle partner, coming down the rope with a self-belay.
3. At a reasonable distance below the middle person (but not close to the crevasse), the free person sets an equalized anchor pair, preferably at least 10 to 15 feet below the middle person, to leave plenty of free rope above the anchor to reach the victim.
4. The free person then loops a three-wrap prusik (or sets an ascender) onto the taut rope leading to the victim, and clips this into the anchor. He then slides this anchoring prusik down the rope until it's fully stretched against the anchor.
5. Now the middle person cautiously moves toward the crevasse, letting the victim's weight go onto the anchor. With the victim solidly anchored, both members can escape from the rope, although they must be wary of other crevasses.

The next step is to assess the victim's condition and position, for these things will determine the nature of the rescue. The victim and the surface members might be able to shout back and forth, but if the victim is any distance down, a surface member will have to go to the crevasse edge to establish communication.

CHECKING THE VICTIM

It should go without saying that anyone venturing near a crevasse into which someone has just fallen needs a belay. More than one would-be rescuer has unwittingly fallen to their death.

Surface members can use another rope or the slack rope "above" the anchor to belay the person going out to check the victim. One surface member can tie off to the anchor and belay another, or a solitary rescuer can go to the lip on a self-belay. If but one rope is available, using a self-belay allows the free end to be sent into the crevasse, either to haul the victim's pack or to rappel on. While approaching the lip, however, it doesn't hurt to back up the self-belay with a figure-eight knot clipped into the harness from slightly farther down the rope. The member going out can also carry one or preferably two ice axes and extra prusiks and runners.

Whatever the belay, it's wise to approach the crevasse lip some distance to the side of where the rope disappears, to avoid putting weight on the unstable lip directly above the victim, as it may break and cause injury. As the surface member approaches the edge, getting down on hands and knees puts less stress on the unstable lip. Then the rescuer can either set the self-belay or instruct the belayer to hold firm while he or she leans out to talk with the victim and assess the situation.

Ideally, the victim is unharmed and either is preparing to ascend the rope or is already doing so. If the victim needs a pack hauled, the free end of the rope can be sent down for this. The person at the lip should wait there to assist the victim over that last desperate overhang. One way to help is to set a prusik or ascender above the lip and use this to lower a ladder of runners for the victim to climb up. Another is simply to reach down with an ice ax for the victim to grab and heave up on.

If a victim cannot ascend out because of injury, partial burial, wedging, or any other reason, then the surface members must haul their partner out. In this case getting the victim past the overhanging remnants of the failed snowbridge can be the hardest part of the task. Preparing for this problem deserves a discussion of its own.

PREPARING CREVASSE LIPS

During a crevasse fall the rope often cuts deeply into the lip, and during hauling the rope saws into it even deeper. As a result, while being hauled the victim rises into the expanse of the overhang, confronting it as a huge barrier. It can be very important for the members at the edge to mitigate this, with either of a couple of different tricks.

First of all, you can slide an ice-ax shaft under the rope and push the rope out to the lip. If the victim is hanging free, you won't be able to push the ax out any farther than the rope already runs. But if there's little or no tension on the rope you should push the ax out as far as the lip will assuredly bear.

If the edge slopes one way or another, then during hauling the rope will slide down the ax shaft. To keep it from sliding off the shaft, place the ax with the adz skyward and on the downhill side of the slope. This way the rope will slide down the shaft to the crotch of the adz and remain there. (Some axes have a sharp edge along the adz shaft joint and should not be used this way.)

Finally, you should tether the ice-ax "pad" to another ax or anchor of some sort away from the lip (see fig. 3.14), because if the ax falls it will invariably fall on the victim. If there's no ax to spare, then a thick cluster of tent poles, a pack, or other items can serve as pads or pad anchors. Ski poles can anchor a pad, but they aren't strong enough to serve as a pad themselves, and if they break their ragged broken edges can slice a rope.

If the rope has already cut too deeply into the lip, the team might have to take a more drastic measure of sending down a "fresh" rope over a prepared and prepadded edge. This is discussed in the next chapter.

Figure 3.14 Padding a crevasse lip (note self-belay and backup)

With the lip prepared one way or another, the final step before setting up a hauling system is to make sure the anchor system is adequate. Most hauling systems multiply the force on the anchor just as they multiply the force on their load, because they depend on creating a tension between anchor and load. The force on the hauling anchor will equal the weight of the victim and gear, plus the friction and resistance at the crevasse lip, multiplied by the pulley system. This is especially dangerous if the victim comes up against the crevasse lip and the haulers continue to pull with all their might; with a pulley system they can generate a tremendous force on both anchor and victim. Therefore, any anchor to be hauled on should be "bombproof."

SETTING UP A HAULING SYSTEM

Once the victim is attached by a prusik to a bombproof anchor, you're ready to set up a hauling system. The most common system is the **three-to-one** or **Z-system**. The Z-system runs the rope through a pulley at the anchor, then up and back through a second pulley attached to the main rope. Essentially it's a C-system except that instead of tying into the anchor the rope runs through the anchor and down to the load. When hauling on this system, the haulers pull in 3 feet of rope for every foot that the victim rises; therefore they have to pull with a force equal to only one-third of the victim's weight, not counting friction. Set up the Z-system like this:

1. *Above* the anchor prusik (that is, on the side away from the victim), push a loop of rope through a belay device. Known as an **autoblock**, this arrangement keeps the anchor prusik from dragging into the pulley placed at the anchor. With an autoblock, the anchoring prusik becomes a ratchet prusik, allowing the haulers to pull the rope through the system, but stopping the rope from sliding back—and the victim from falling back. When the rope is hauled through the pulley, the prusik jams against the plate and lets the rope run freely. When the rope lets out, the prusik stretches tight and reanchors it.
2. Immediately *above* the autoblock, thread the rope through a pulley, and clip this pulley into the anchor with a new carabiner (see fig. 3.15a).
3. From this pulley at the anchor, loop the rope back parallel to itself as far up toward the crevasse as it's safe to go, and thread the slack line through another pulley.
4. Wrap and set a prusik around the main strand.

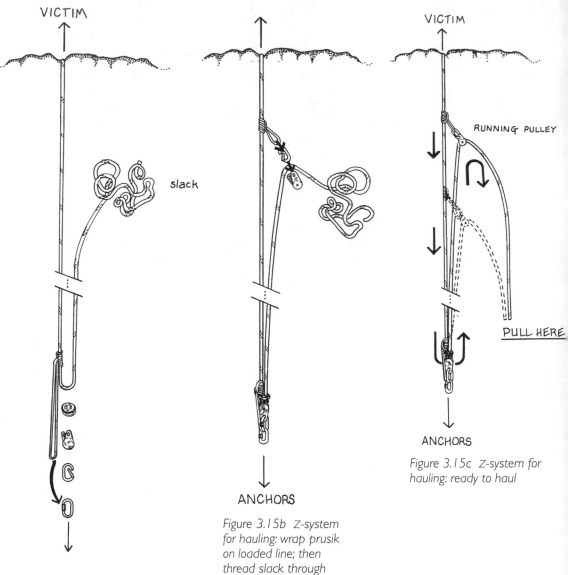

VICTIM

slack

VICTIM

RUNNING PULLEY

VICTIM

PULL HERE

ANCHORS

Figure 3.15c Z-system for hauling: ready to haul

ANCHORS

Figure 3.15b Z-system for hauling: wrap prusik on loaded line; then thread slack through pulley and clip to prusik

Figure 3.15a Z-system for hauling: thread rope through belay plate (autoblock), then pulley, then clip pulley to anchor (note: prusik is already taut to anchor carabiner, holding weight of victim)

5. Clip the new pulley into the new prusik (see fig. 3.15b), and run the slack line back to the anchor. This is the line you haul with, and you're now ready to haul (see fig. 3.15c).

There are a number of other methods for creating a ratchet at the anchor in a hauling system, all with advantages and disadvantages. Among the useful ones are the Garda hitch, the Penberthy knot, and the French braid. I won't attempt to describe these alternatives, but for those who might be introduced to them I will compare their important features.

The **Garda hitch** has the advantage of offering an immediate brake with no slack. However, because no pulley is used, it generates added friction. Also, its simple but crucial construction is easy to forget.

The **Penberthy knot** and the **French braid** both offer fairly quick brakes, but only slightly or no better than a prusik with an autoblock. Depending on the pulley and perlon used and the tying method, these two ratchet systems can jam into the pulley, adding significant friction or dangerously stopping the pulley.

Gear-minded climbers can buy "prusik-minding" pulleys with flanges for keeping a prusik or related knot away from the wheel, an integral autoblock. Most function okay, but still need tending. Also available are pulleys with an ascender-like cam that serves as a ratchet. Although manufacturers warn that these cams damage the rope in shock-load falls, they seem safe and convenient for crevasse rescue hauling.

Because the prusik-autoblock setup offers excellent performance using gear generally carried anyway, for most teams it remains the recommended method.

IMPROVISATION

It was the first working day of an expedition to climb Nun in Kashmir. Our team and a handful of porters had crossed some snowfields to cache our supplies where we thought the glacier began. One of the porters punched a foot through where there'd been no sign of a crevasse, so we knew the warm conditions were dangerous.

As the last four of us were returning to base camp, a Japanese climber trying an adjacent peak yelled down from the edge of another glacier. One of his buddies had fallen into a crevasse. He was three meters down. Could we help? Most of our gear was hours away at our cache, but we just happened to have with us one harness, four carabiners, two ascenders, two axes and some webbing. We had no rope, no anchors, and no pulleys.

We followed the panicked Japanese leader to the crevasse. There was no sign of his partner, for he had fallen much deeper than three meters, without a rope or harness. The leader said he had a rope and tent cached about 20 minutes away. These items were the only hope. I followed their footsteps, probing constantly and gasping as I occasionally found hollowness. But in not quite an hour I returned with the rope and tent poles. We buried the poles for an anchor and backed that up with a buried ax. Giving the Japanese leader our ascenders and spare harness, we lowered him into the crevasse, insisting on double assurance that he knew how to ascend back out.

A long time went by with no word from below. We yelled down, but the leader's English had crumbled into incomprehensible murmurs. By then a squall came in, and with snow collecting on us we started shivering and thinking about the approaching night. I decided to haul out the leader, and if the original victim was a goner, so be it. With two carabiners and a runner in a kleimheist knot, I built an inefficient Z-system. With our first heave, such a blood-curdling wail erupted out of the crevasse that we figured the rope was somehow wrapped around a tender organ. We stopped hauling and went back to waiting.

Another 20 minutes went by, and I decided, organs or no, we had to pull this guy out and get back to camp. We hauled, the screams resumed, and we kept hauling. We had no ratchet at the anchor, so when it was time to reset the running kleimheist I pinched the rope bend at the anchor carabiner with all my might, while another slid the knot and running carabiner back toward the crevasse. Still bellowing, the leader reached the surface, the ascenders clamped on the rope but unused.

"Your buddy?" we asked.

"Yes. Ready for rescue."

We switched to the other end of the rope, and hauled out the original victim. He was cold, and the long slide down a narrow chimney had beaten up his hand, but other than that he was fine.

After 10 years of climbing and half as many guiding, I looked at the various levels of competence around me, and I was glad I had been given the caution, and learned the skills, to avoid such situations.

HAULING

Hauling itself is a straightforward matter of pulling on the free strand of the rope, in line with the anchor and victim. Added security and power can come from the haulers tying into the rope and pulling from their harnesses, rather than just holding the rope with their hands.

During hauling, the second or "running" pulley moves toward the anchor pulley. Depending on how far the victim needs to be hauled and how far you set the running pulley out from the anchor, you'll probably bring this running pulley up to the anchor. At this point you need to carefully let the victim's weight back onto the ratchet prusik, perhaps stretching out this prusik manually to make doubly sure it immediately grabs.

Here it also doesn't hurt to check that the ratchet prusik isn't getting significantly abraded from the haul rope. In rare cases, mainly on an icy ablation zone where grit can coat the rope, the ratchet prusik can abrade quickly. Once the victim's weight is securely held by the ratchet prusik, you can slide the running pulley and its prusik back down the taut primary rope as far as is practical, and then resume hauling.

As the victim approaches an overhanging lip it's *imperative* that the haulers slow down, then stop hauling before heaving the victim into the lip. It's surprisingly easy to haul a victim into an overhang, embedding the person there as a human fluke. Assuming that the ratchet prusik holds as tightly as it should, the victim will then be in a very serious predicament with no reasonable way to move up or down.

To haul over a lip requires coordination between haulers and victim, for the victim will have to knock away the lip and push away from it; only then can the haulers heave another foot or two. In this way a team hauls around and over a lip in small increments. Of course, this takes communication between the haulers and the victim, and for this reason it's best if a surface member remains at the lip to relay signals. If there's no spare rope for the relayer to tie-in to the main anchor, a personal anchor can be set up a short distance away from the lip. Another workable option is for the relayer to simply keep a waist prusik on the haul rope as a self-belay. If no relayer can be spared, then the haulers must be extremely wary of any increase in the resistance as they haul, and they must yell back and forth with the victim as best as they can. In chapter 4, the section "Building in a Tension-Release Mechanism" describes a system that allows a victim to be lowered from implantation into an overhang.

Here's a summary of the bare minimum of gear used to set up the Z-system:

2 prusiks or mechanical ascenders
2 anchors
2 pulleys
1 ice ax, but preferably 2 ice axes
1 long runner or cordelette
6 or 7 carabiners

Therefore, in order to make up for gear that will go into a crevasse with a victim, a party of three should carry at least 50 percent more of each of these items, equally distributed among the members. Parties on glaciers with more serious crevasse hazards are wise to carry more anchors, runners, cordelettes, and carabiners. The latter three can be most valuable, for they allow a team to bury and equalize deadman anchors from almost anything, and runners can also substitute for prusiks when tied in a **kleimheist knot** (see Appendix 2). If the team is in a pinch for pulleys, the rope can simply be looped through carabiners instead, but of course the greater friction makes hauling much more difficult.

LOWERING A VICTIM WITH THE HAULING SYSTEM

There can be reasons to lower a victim deeper into a crevasse; most obviously if lowering gets the victim to a place where walking or climbing out of the crevasse is feasible. Another reason is to lower a victim onto a fresh strand, which is described in the next chapter under "Rescuing Over a Newly Prepared Lip." The key step in lowering a victim is to temporarily deactivate the ratchet prusik (or ascender) at the anchor. This requires that you haul the victim up a short distance, and then carefully let rope out through the haul system. The procedure is as follows:

1. Build a Z-system as previously described, and then haul the victim just enough to take all the weight off the ratchet prusik.
2. One surface member must hold the wraps of the ratchet prusik open, while another can lower the victim by slowly letting rope out through the haul system. (One person can do both, if necessary.)
3. If the victim needs to be lowered a fair distance, make sure the running pulley of the Z-system doesn't run too far. When this pulley has run a reasonable distance, the rescuer at the anchor resets the ratchet prusik. Then the lowering rescuer can go out to retrieve the running pulley and slide it back close to the anchor. This procedure can be repeated to lower the victim as far as the amount of free rope allows.

MIDDLE PERSON IN

Contrary to what one might think, a climber in the middle of a rope team can fall a good distance into a crevasse. Even though a middle person has a rope on both sides, it's not uncommon for both ropes to be slack or oblique to crevasses. And rescuing a middle person actually can be more problematic.

When a person in the interior of a four-person rope team breaks through a snowbridge, the two surface members who are together on one side of the crevasse are best situated to carry out the rescue. Their procedures are the same as when a member on the end of a three-person rope goes in; the adjacent member holds the weight and the end member sets an anchor "below" them.

However, when the middle person on a three-person team falls into a crevasse, the two end members must hold the fall and then shout back and forth across the crevasse to decide which of them is holding most of the weight. The procedure then runs as follows:

1. The free member goes toward the victim on a self-belay, preferably coming far enough to generate adequate slack to reach the victim.
2. This rescuer sets an anchor and connects it to the rope with a prusik.
3. Next the rescuer travels on a self-belay to the crevasse edge to pad the lip under the rope.
4. Now the weight-bearing member across the crevasse eases toward the victim, letting the weight swing onto the other surface member's anchor.
5. The rescuer at the lip who set the anchor can now initiate the rescue, if necessary sending the slack rope down to haul the victim's pack, waiting to assist the prusiking victim over the lip, or setting up a pulley system to haul the victim out (see fig. 3.16).

OTHER HAULING SYSTEMS

The Z-system has proven to be the most versatile for hauling crevasse victims and it should be the method of first choice in most cases. In fact, knowing more ways to haul can be a burden because in a tense situation rescuers can lose valuable time deciding which method to use, and different methods can even be confused with one another. However, the following three methods can offer a faster rescue in some cases.

Straight pull. When there are perhaps five or more rescuers available, and the lip is not problematic or has been well prepared, rescuers can usually just directly haul the victim out. Those hauling should either tie into the rope or pull with a prusik or ascender from their harnesses, to make sure that they don't drop the victim. One member must be ready to hold open the anchor prusik as the rescuers haul.

C-pulley. The simple two-to-one pulley system used to describe pulley theory earlier in this chapter also can be used to haul a victim.

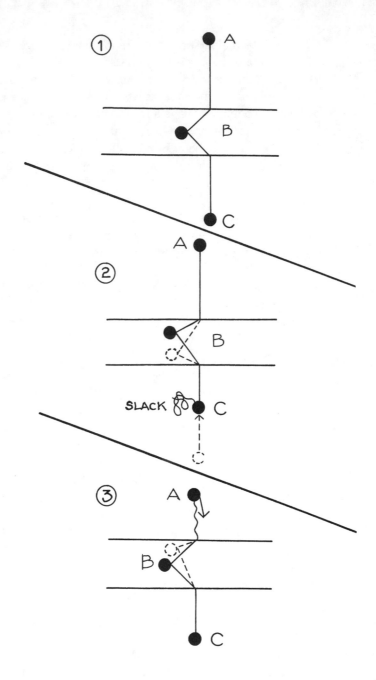

Figure 3.16 Middle person in, schematic sequence: top, B falls in; middle, A holds weight, C sets anchor, generating slack; bottom, A releases B onto anchor, C rescues

1. Assuming the victim's rope is anchored off with a prusik, thread the slack rope "above" the prusik through a pulley.
2. Clip a carabiner, preferably a locking model, into this pulley. Send the pulley and carabiner to the victim on a loop of rope, holding on to the slack end of the rope.
3. After the victim clips the pulley with its loop of rope to his or her harness, begin to haul on the end you have been holding onto.

This system is good for a quick and easy haul when the victim is just a few feet into the crevasse, but unable to heave out. This is a common situation, when a victim gets stuck in a partially collapsed bridge or gets wedged between crevasse walls. This system strains the anchor much less than does a Z-system, because the friction at the lip bears mostly on the haulers' strand. A disadvantage of the C-system is that it can't be easily rigged with a ratcheting belay.

Bilgeri. The bilgeri was the method of choice before prusik ascending came into use, and it still has some fans. It involves running two ropes for the victim to tie loops with and stand in, one for each foot. Each rope is connected to a surface anchor by a prusik. The victim shifts his or her weight to one rope while the rescuer pulls up on the other and alternates ropes until the victim reaches the surface. In practice, rope stretch and spinning make this system more difficult, less secure, and slower than ascending or hauling.

HYPOTHERMIC VICTIMS

During a prolonged rescue, crevasse victims often become severely chilled or hypothermic. This condition is not unlike shock. It begins when, in response to cold, the body shunts blood away from the periphery and sequesters it for the internal organs. With prolonged cold even the body's core cools down, and this changes the blood chemistry, drops the metabolism, and generally compromises the organs, especially the heart. A severely hypothermic victim is at great risk of heart failure, especially from jostling of the heart. More than one crevasse victim has died after reaching the surface and apparent safety for mysterious but probably related reasons.

Rescuers should thus take whatever care they can to avoid jarring the victim. Once the victim is out of the crevasse, minimize stress and preserve what little blood flow to the organs there is. Immediately lay the victim down and elevate the feet. Then take care to rewarm the person gradually. Warm fluids can be very helpful, but the most effective treatment is insulated warm (not hot) water bottles around the torso or the old body-to-body contact in a sleeping bag.

Of course, the best solution is to prevent hypothermia in the first place. The seriousness of getting too cold is a good incentive to have clothing handy, and to have rescue procedures down pat.

HUMILITY

A year after the Kashmir trip I was assigned to teach a basic mountaineering course on the Kahiltna Glacier, below Denali in Alaska. Right after landing on the glacier, I taught my two students the fundamentals of glacier travel and crevasse rescue. A point I emphasized more than once was that any incidents would have to be dealt with immediately by our party. Help would be too far away.

About the fifth day into the course, I found an ice slope suitable for practicing crampon techniques. It was wind-scoured, blue ice at a low angle, perfect for learning. I knew we wouldn't be in danger of crevasses here, so on the easy ground I led us around without the rope. We progressed to some steeper places, and by afternoon I returned to the easy area to demonstrate chopping steps.

Unroped, I walked out a narrow ledge with a coating of snow on it. Suddenly I was falling, plummeting in a chaos of snow and ice. Whump! I came to a stop 30 feet down. Never in a hundred years would I have guessed that that ledge was a covered crevasse, but how instantly was I proven clueless! I wrestled one arm free, and my head was free, but my buried legs and an arm (still gripping my ax) were held fast, like a bug in amber. Wow, an instant panic seized me to get out as fast as possible. I knew I was lucky, and that my students would soon come to my rescue. I yelled.

Twenty minutes later I was still yelling, scraping futilely with my one free arm, but starting to shiver and starting to worry. Thankfully I had overdressed for the hot day above, but I did not have hours. Why were they taking so long to even look into the hole? All they had to do was set a couple screws like we'd just practiced, tie off the rope and come over. It turned out that they were arguing over whether or not to go search for help. Luckily the doctor of the pair held the day, and after half an hour I heard a timid voice from the daylight above me.

I yelled for them to lower me an ice ax and a jacket, and 15 minutes later that package came down to my waving grasp. I chopped myself free, confirmed they'd anchored the rope, and then prusiked out. Looking back down, I saw that the soft shelf I'd landed in was only fifteen feet long; farther along, the slot was perfectly black.

Back in the warm tent, I evaluated my mistake. How many hundreds of crevasses had I come across, always roped? Crevasse caution had been my middle name for years, but there I was, as fooled as any novice and living testimony to the wonders of chance. How much had I set my trust on instincts, and how accurate were those instincts? Even though I thought I'd long before sorted out the proper zone between caution and confidence, clearly I still had blind spots. I could only give thanks that I had another chance.

CHAPTER 4
ADDITIONAL RESCUE TECHNIQUES

For those new to mountain rescue techniques, it's usually enough of a challenge to first learn the procedural outline of crevasse rescue and the basic methods described in chapter 3. However, crevasse rescues can demand more than what can be accomplished with those basic techniques. Therefore, this chapter advances a rescuer's repertoire with techniques designed to prevent or solve complex crevasse-rescue problems, techniques that integrate with the basic procedures of the previous chapter.

ADDITIONAL HAULING POWER: THE ZxC

The three-to-one Z-system typically requires at least two and often three haulers to get one person out of a crevasse, depending on their strength, the victim's weight, and, especially, the amount of friction at the lip. If for any reason you need more hauling power, you can most easily get it by adding a two-to-one C-system onto the Z. This is the ZxC. The fairly simple procedure goes like this:

1. Take the free end of the rope coming off the Z-system (or the end of an entirely new rope) and fix it to the anchor.
2. Wrap a prusik on the hauling strand of the Z-system just "above" the running pulley.
3. Feed the newly tied line through a pulley and clip this pulley to the new prusik. Bring the line back toward the anchor, and you're ready to haul again on this strand (see fig. 4.1).

The two-to-one C-pulley subsystem doubles the Z's mechanical advantage to six to one; usually this is enough for one person to haul out even a heavy victim. Hauling with this system goes slowly, for the victim's strand comes in only one-sixth as fast as the haulers take in rope. The third pulley is a second running pulley, and it will come up against the

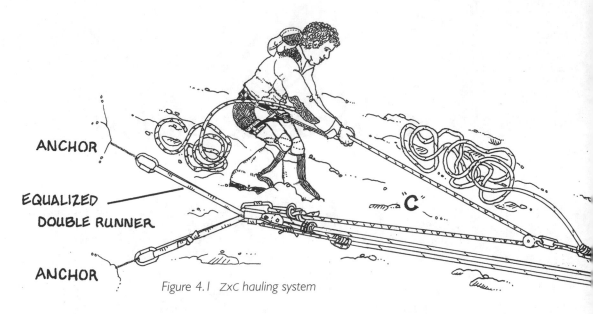

ANCHOR

EQUALIZED
DOUBLE RUNNER

ANCHOR

C

Figure 4.1 *ZxC hauling system*

anchor and have to be reset twice as often as the Z's original running pulley.

THE CANADIAN DROP LOOP SYSTEM

Guides and rescue teams in Canada often favor the Canadian drop loop system, a variation of the 6:1 haul system, because tests show it exerts 40 percent less force on the anchor. Also, because a fresh rope strand is sent to the victim, it is easy to set up good padding to prevent the rope from slicing into the crevasse lip. The primary disadvantage is that the victim must be conscious and accessible to a rope throw.

Start building the system by sending a loop of rope from the anchor down to the victim; the victim clips the loop into a pulley and attaches this to his or her harness. Now you run the strand coming back from the victim through an autoblock and ratchet at the anchor. Run the rope back toward the victim and through a pulley with a prusik on the strand coming up from the victim, and you're ready to haul. Essentially you've built a Z-system onto a C-system on the victim (see fig. 4.2).

This system requires more rope, so if only one rope is available the rescuer who sets the anchor will want to set it a good distance "below" the rescuer holding the victim to generate extra slack. Most parties of two with only one rope will not have enough to build this system.

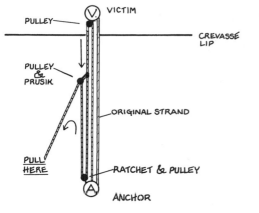

CANADIAN DROP LOOP SYSTEM

Figure 4.2 Schematic of Canadian drop loop system

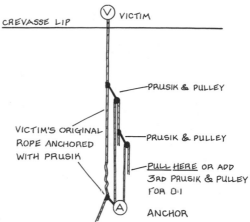

Figure 4.3 Schematic of Windless 4:1

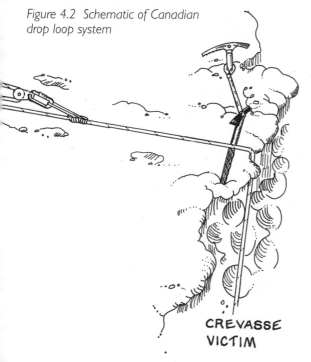

CREVASSE
VICTIM

MÜNTER
HITCH

Figure 4.4 Münter hitch

THE WINDLASS 4:1 OR 8:1

Essentially a double or triple C-system, the windlass 4:1 or 8:1 gets more hauling power out of two or three pulleys, and if a spare rope is available it's quick to set up (see fig. 4.3). A disadvantage is that the anchoring ratchet must be worked manually.

1. With the victim's rope anchored with a prusik and the anchors backed up, fix the end of the new hauling rope to the anchor.
2. At a good but safe distance down the victim's strand, tie a three-wrap prusik onto the victim's strand, and then connect this prusik to a bend in the new hauling strand with a pulley.
3. A long distance down the hauling line (perhaps at the middle), fix the hauling line to the anchor again and repeat the prusik/pulley arrangement on the first hauling strand.

This generates a 4:1 system. Note that the victim's original strand is not pulled through the anchoring prusik, and so one of the rescuers must pull the slack that develops in the victim's line through this anchor prusik. At the very least a rescuer will have to pull it through and set the prusik when it's time to reset the pulleys or check the victim's progress.

For an 8:1 you can build a third C onto the hauling strand in this system.

BUILDING IN A TENSION-RELEASE MECHANISM

A tension-release mechanism allows rescuers to lower a victim, which several different situations can call for. Most simply, some crevasses allow victims to walk or climb out once they are lowered to the "floor." More critically, if a victim is inadvertently hauled into an overhang, it can be crucial to lower the person enough to clear the overhang. A third reason to lower a victim is to transfer to a new rope to circumvent a blocking overhang.

When anchoring off the victim, the basic concept of the tension-release mechanism is to extend the anchor prusik and wrap this extension through a friction brake. The most compact friction brake to use here is a **Münter hitch** (see fig. 1.1), which is then tied off. The procedure described here fits in the "Anchoring the Rope" section in chapter 3 when a rescuer is ready to connect the victim's rope to an anchor with a prusik:

1. Clip a locking carabiner (preferably a large Münter'biner) into the anchor, and wrap a prusik onto the victim's rope with a cordelette.
2. Pull the extra cord snug and tie it into a Münter hitch on the

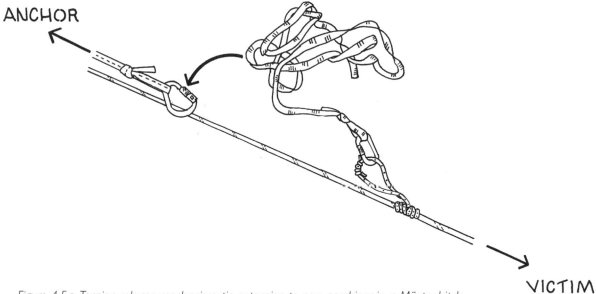

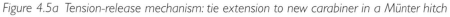

Figure 4.5a Tension-release mechanism: tie extension to new carabiner in a Münter hitch

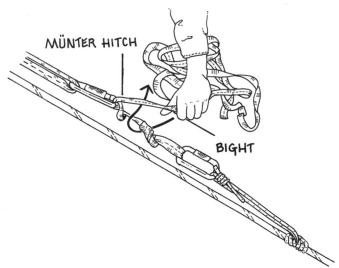

Figure 4.5b Tension-release mechanism: tie off Münter hitch (half hitch)

locking carabiner.

3. Tie off the Münter hitch with a half hitch, and then an overhand knot (full hitch). As a final backup, knot the very end of the

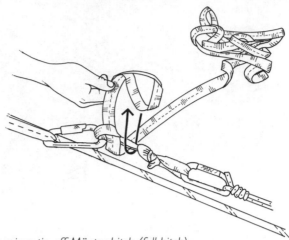

Figure 4.5c Tension-release mechanism: tie off Münter hitch (full hitch)

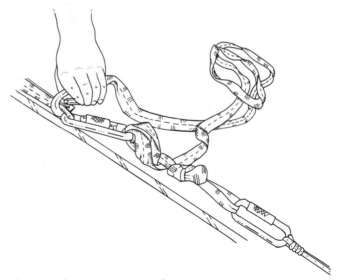

Figure 4.5d Tension-release mechanism: clip extension to anchor

cordelette and clip it to the anchor. You can use the cordelette as a single strand, tying a large loop at the end of the cord and wrap-ping the prusik with this loop. Then you tie the Münter with a single strand and have extra length to lower the victim. Or, you can use the cordelette in its usual loop, wrap the prusik using the entire cordelette, and tie the Münter with a double strand. You can also use a normal prusik loop and tie the Münter with an extension of webbing as in fig. 4.5.

4. Now you can proceed with the rescue as previously described. The rescuer holding the victim can release the load onto the Münter hitch and anchor. To set up a hauling system, start with another carabiner on the anchor, and clip the pulley with its autoblock and the rope into this.

5. To lower the victim, undo the full hitch and, while holding firm on the Münter, pull out the half hitch. Now you can carefully let out the Münter, which will lower the victim. The Münter hitch is a high-friction brake, and lowering a victim over a crevasse lip will not be a problem. When the victim is lowered far enough, retie the half and full hitches.

6. For hauling, you'll probably want to get the anchor (ratchet) prusik back close to the anchor before retying the hitches. To do this, have others (if available) hold the victim's weight via the haul system while you slide the ratchet prusik back and pull the extension back through the Münter, and then retie the backup knots. With the anchor prusik back near the anchor, you can lower the victim again if necessary.

A tension-release mechanism can be added into a haul system even if you have fixed the original anchoring prusik to the anchor, as described earlier. To do this, wrap a new ratchet prusik onto the victim's strand and add the Münter extension onto a fresh (locking) carabiner at the anchor. Build the haul system and haul just enough to take the weight off the original prusik, which you can then unclip and remove. Now the tension-release prusik is also the main ratchet prusik.

To those who are relatively new to rescue techniques, building a tension-release mechanism can seem a complicated and confusing addition. Indeed, it is not worth doing and dangerous to attempt if the rescuers don't understand the principles and know the procedure well. However, for those with experience, the tension-release mechanism simply inserts a proven belay into the victim's anchor attachment, and with practice the mechanism can be added in less than half a minute.

RESCUING OVER A NEWLY PREPARED LIP

As noted earlier, the rope can cut very deeply into the lip during a crevasse fall, and getting the victim past a great eave can pose a major obstacle. The surest way to solve the problem is by sending down a fresh rope over a prepared and prepadded edge off to the side of where the original rope has cut in. When clearing away a large overhang, however, great care has to be taken to avoid bombarding the victim with blocks of snow. The surface member who goes out to check the victim should decide if cultivating a new edge is necessary. If it is, the procedure then goes as follows:

1. Build a Z or ZxC haul system on the victim's original rope and haul the person to within a few feet of the overhang. This gets the victim out of the way of falling debris and generates more slack.

2. To the side of the original rope, far enough away to keep the victim clear, knock away the lip and set a rope pad as described in chapter 3, "Preparing Crevasse Lips."

3. Send the "fresh" strand of rope down for the victim to tie into, then run it over the newly prepared lip site. It will be easier to use an entirely different rope if one is available, although sending down the other end of the victim's original strand works fine if it's your only rope.

4. Connect the fresh strand to the anchor with a prusik, and pull the slack out of the rope and prusik.

5. Lower the victim on the original haul line until the person's weight swings onto the new strand, using one of two methods. As described earlier, you can lower with the original haul system. Alternatively, if you have built a tension-release hitch into your ratchet prusik, you can untie the backup hitches and lower the victim out with the Münter hitch.

6. Using the newly weighted strand, either the victim can ascend out of the crevasse or surface members can haul the person out by breaking down the original haul system and building a new one on the fresh strand. Once the victim's weight is completely off the original strand, the victim should untie from it to avoid getting it snagged in the overhang.

TWO-PERSON PARTIES

As mentioned earlier, traveling on a glacier with just one partner begets the serious possibility of one person having to rescue another. For this reason, the traditional wisdom has been "never travel with fewer than three." But this is too restricting for many people. Indeed, many parties travel across glaciers in order to reach a technical climb, where the most efficient team will be a pair. Also, it can be hard enough to gather even one partner with the time, ability, and interest to take a trip, much less

"You can look down in [the crevasses] for distances stretching from your feet to Hades or China. Look down one of them and you never will forget it... most of them appear to be bottomless. These are not good things to look at."

—Tom Lloyd during (unroped) first
ascent of Mount McKinley, 1910. From
The Sourdough Expedition. Terrence Cole.

two or more. But while the temptations for going onto a glacier with just one partner are clear, they make it easy to overlook the central question: Do pairs really have the "safety net"—the rescue backup—that they need?

A party of two *can* have a reasonable safety net if they are cautious about the crevasses they cross and if they are very competent at rescue technique. In fact, it can be safer to travel with one competent partner than with any number of incompetent partners. However, while one competent individual can perform most crevasse rescue procedures, roped pairs need to understand that the most basic element of initiating a crevasse rescue can be very difficult for *any* one person: setting an anchor.

When one climber holds a partner's crevasse fall, very often the partner's weight continues to bear down. The surface member must set an anchor while holding this weight (mitigated by friction of the rope over the crevasse lip). Too few glacier travelers have given much thought to the need to set an anchor while holding a person's weight, much less practiced it. But imagine holding your partner's crevasse fall and *not* anchoring off. Do you just lie there in ice-ax arrest and hope the victim can prusik out, while both your lives depend on your grip in the snow? How long do you wait?

Pairs should keep at least two anchors appropriate to the conditions very handy, ideally clipped to their harnesses or low on the shoulder straps of their packs. They should also have prusiks on the rope (or ascenders *very* handy), for these are what will connect the taut rope to the anchor. Remember, too, that each partner should travel with enough slack rope to reach the other. Now, assume the worst case: you've had to hold a fall with an ice-ax arrest. From here your procedure is as follows:

1. Work from the ice-ax arrest position to a position that allows you to still hold the victim's weight but free at least one hand to set an anchor. Usually the key is to dig in your feet and bear as much of the load with them as possible. One good compromise position is to roll onto one leg and brace with the other, perhaps still holding

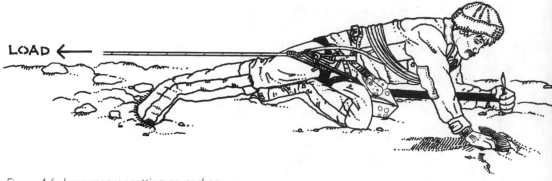

LOAD ←

Figure 4.6 Lone rescuer setting an anchor

onto the ice ax. The pose looks something like a baseball player sliding into home plate (see fig. 4.6). If the victim's weight bears heavily, you might have to stay generally prone in ice-ax arrest.

2. Assuming the anchor of choice is a fluke, scour out a T-shaped trench, as similar as possible to the ideal trench described in chapter 3. If you've been successful at taking most of the weight with your feet, you might be able to dig with your ice ax. Otherwise, you'll have to dig with your hand or perhaps a second ice tool. Gauge the site of the trench so that when you set the fluke, the extensions of your prusiks or ascenders will just reach the fluke's carabiner. If you've been traveling with a Texas prusik system on the rope, dig the fluke's trench at about shoulder level, and the stirrup loops should barely reach the fluke's carabiner.

3. Set the fluke and give it a few test yanks.

4. Connect the fluke to the rope with a prusik or ascender. Here we see another bonus of traveling with the Texas system on the rope, because the stirrup loops can be pulled out and immediately clipped to the fluke.

5. Ease back toward the crevasse, keeping a watchful eye on the fluke. The victim's weight transfers onto the fluke as you back away. Be ready to jump back into ice-ax arrest should this primary anchor fail.

6. When the primary anchor obviously holds all the victim's weight, unclip from the rope and add a backup anchor (as described in chapter 3). Make sure there's a minimum of slack in the connecting runner. With the rope anchored off, rescue procedures are the same as for larger parties, except there are fewer options.

7. With a self-belay on the slack rope you've been carrying, go to the lip and check your buddy's condition. If he or she needs a pack

hauled up, you can send down the remaining free rope and yank it up hand over hand. If the victim can then ascend out without assistance, you can wait at the lip to help heave the person over it. If the victim absolutely needs your assistance to be freed or for first aid, then you can pad the lip and go down immediately, taking the necessary clothing and gear.

8. If your partner needs to be hauled, do what you can to prepare the lip under the rope without bombarding the person with blocks of snow.

9. Go back to your anchors and build a six-to-one (ZxC) pulley system, preferably with a tension-release hitch. While hauling, remain very sensitive to any increase in resistance, because there's no one to relay warnings when your buddy is coming to an overhang, and if injured there's no one to assist him or her over. When you do feel added resistance, stop hauling and give your buddy a chance to knock away an eave or push away from it.

10. When you suspect you've pulled your partner up to the final lip, it's wise to run out to the edge and make sure you're going to be able to haul over it. Go out on a self-belay set on the main rescue line. You might need to carefully knock away as much of the overhang as possible now; with your partner close to the lip, it will be safer to knock away hunks of snow. How much of a lip you can haul over depends on how capable the victim is to help, and how deeply the rope cuts into the lip.

11. Once the lip is certainly surmountable, return to the haul system and heave your buddy up.

If the rope knifes very deeply into the lip, and/or if the victim is too injured to help much, you might have to haul over a new site to the side. Without rescue partners this is difficult, but without someone at the lip to help an incapacitated victim, hauling over even a small eave can prove impossible. The new-site procedure is basically the same as when there are two or more rescuers:

1. When you've hauled to near the final overhang, put a self-belay on the free strand of rope, and go out to the lip. To the side of where your buddy dangles, prepare the new haul site.

2. Send down the free end of the rope for your partner to tie into, and then run the strand over the newly prepared site.

3. Go back to the haul system and anchor off the "new" strand with a prusik, pulling all the slack out of this strand.

4. Then lower the victim so the person's weight comes fully onto the

new strand. If you rigged your haul system with a tension-release hitch, you can probably lower out enough with this. If not, you can lower with the haul system as described earlier in this chapter, holding the ratchet prusik open yourself.

5. Break down the first haul system and build a new one on the fresh strand. Now you're ready to haul over the freshly prepared site.

Clearly, with a lone rescuer the rescue for any crevasse fall is both involved and uncertain; thus two-person parties should travel and cross crevasses more conservatively than a larger group might. Pairs should realize that even if they are practiced at rescue procedures, setting an anchor and hauling past a large lip are weak links in their safety net. Of course, each member of a pair needs to carry enough gear to rescue the other: at least two anchors for any conditions expected, preferably three pulleys, and also extra runners, carabiners, and prusiks.

TYING OFF A BELAY (SLIP HITCH)

When members of a two-person party decide to belay across a fragile-looking crevasse bridge, and the bridge fails, the belayer will have to hold the fall and then "tie off" the belay. With hands then freed, the rescuer can anchor off the rope. The tie-off knot is the same as described for the Münter tie-off. Assuming you hold the fall with a belay plate in an anchored-sitting belay, here's the general procedure. Depending on the harness, you may need to tie the hitches "above" the belay plate, around the loaded strand.

1. With one hand, hold the rope back from the belay plate to maintain the friction that holds the victim's weight. With the free hand, bring a bight of rope from the brake hand around the harness loop, and pass the bight under the loop created (see fig. 4.7a). This is the tie-off half hitch.

2. Still holding the brake strand, pull plenty of slack into the bight, and pull out all of the slack between the brake hand and the bight. Hold onto the bight and let go with the brake hand. The weight of the victim will tighten the half hitch (see fig. 4.7b).

3. Tie the bight around the harness strand in a whole hitch, the tie-off backup (see fig. 4.7c).

4. Now you are free to connect the rope to the anchor, as in any crevasse rescue situation. Wrap a prusik around the load rope and clip the prusik to the anchor. Ease toward the victim, letting the person's weight come onto the prusik and anchor. Now you can untie the hitches at your harness and carry out a rescue.

CLIMBER

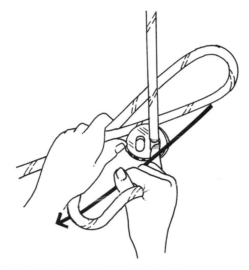

Figure 4.7a Tying off a belay: hold belay and tie half hitch around harness loop

CLIMBER

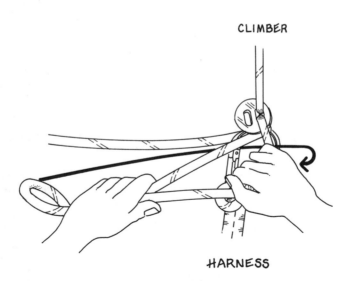

HARNESS

Figure 4.7b Tying off a belay: pull out slack between brake hand and half hitch

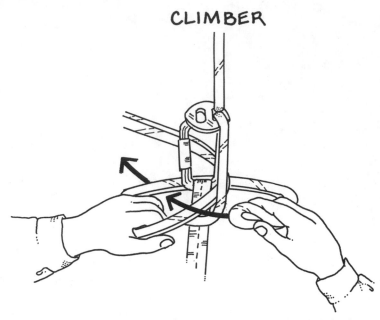

CLIMBER

Figure 4.7c Tying off a belay: tie bight around harness loop in whole hitch

RAPPELLING TO AID A VICTIM

What do you do when you go out to the crevasse lip and there's a labored, pained response, or no response? Is the victim hanging limp? Is there a pack? A chest harness? Can you even see where he or she stopped? Do you go down to help? If the victim is severely injured, severely hypothermic or unconscious, going down could be the only way to save a life. On the other hand, the time it takes for someone to go down and administer to a victim suffering only slightly can be time enough to have them suffering severely, and putting a second person in a crevasse is not to be taken lightly.

Decisions like these cannot be covered with blanket statements, and in rescue situations often too little is known to say with certainty that a given decision will be the right one.

To help, it's important to know what conditions can put a crevasse victim in mortal danger. Hypothermia is probably the most common trauma that crevasse rescuers can do much about. Severe bleeding is another case in which rescuers might save a person's life by going down immediately. More mechanically, victims often get wedged between crevasse walls or swamped in snow, and need help getting free. A problem inherent to vertical rescues arises when victims hang unconscious, because typically their lax tongues slump over their airways, and in this condition a victim likely will suffocate in minutes.

Whatever the reason to go down, in rescue terminology the person going down to aid the victim is the **third man**. It's preferable for the third man to go down on a completely fresh rope, keeping the slack part of the victim's rope available for a hauling system. But let's assume a three-person party with only one rope:

1. With luck, the victim's strand was originally anchored as much as 15 to 20 feet down from the rope's center, for this will allow enough slack to build a Z-pulley system and to rappel on. The anchor should be backed up for a second person's weight.
2. Tie the rappel strand to the anchor not quite 15 feet along the slack side from the rope's center (it pays to have the middle of your rope marked). This should leave you enough rope to reach the victim, and about 30 to 40 feet of slack to set up a Z-system on the victim's strand.
3. Gather the supplies you'll need for administering first aid, for keeping the victim and you warm, and for chopping or digging, as well as slings and prusiks for rigging support, as described in the next section. Remember prusiks or ascenders to get yourself back out!
4. Go to the lip, away from where the victim's rope disappears, and prepare a site over which to rappel.
5. Wrap a prusik around the rappel strand and clip it to your harness. This will be your brake upon reaching the victim. As you rappel, hold the prusik wraps open, bringing the prusik down with you.
6. As you rappel to just barely above the victim, halt your rappel by letting go of the prusik wraps and settling onto the prusik.
7. Take off the victim's pack and clip it out of the way. Administer first aid, free the victim from wedging or snow burial, or whatever else needs to be done.
8. Tell your partner on the surface to set up a haul system and prepare to haul.
9. Ascend with the victim as your partner proceeds to haul the person up.

This basic sequence of third man procedures has omitted the most technical consideration, because it deserves a discussion of its own: making sure that the victim, especially if unconscious or semiconscious, hangs with his or her head upright, and as comfortably as possible (see fig. 4.8a to c). Here the third man's crucial job is to rig support for the

Figure 4.8a Improvising support for an unconscious victim: rigging a chest harness

Figure 4.8b Improvising support for an unconscious victim: an improvised C-pulley allows victim's torso to be raised and clipped into supported position

Figure 4.8c Improvising support for an unconscious victim: use prusik and runner to support victim's legs

victim's torso and head, keeping the head tilted back to keep the airway open. A conscious but badly injured victim or a hypothermic victim who might go unconscious should be given this support during a rescue. However, even an experienced climber will need practice to get this procedure down:

1. As you hang off a waist prusik just above the victim, rig a chest harness on the victim (see fig. 4.8a).
2. Put a prusik or ascender on the rope the victim hangs from.
3. Clip a runner to the prusik and run this through a carabiner on the chest harness; this carabiner then acts as an improvised C-pulley, and you can raise the victim's torso by pulling the runner back up to the prusik (see fig. 4.8b). Without this "pulley" it will be virtually impossible to raise the victim's torso. Set the prusik so that the victim's torso will hang from it at a slight incline, and then clip this other end of the runner into the prusik.
4. With another runner padded by an article of clothing, support the victim's neck and head, clipping this runner to another prusik or perhaps the same one as for the chest harness. Make sure the victim's head is supported but tilted back to keep the airway open.
5. If necessary support the victim's legs with another prusik and a runner or two (see fig. 4.8c).

Clearly, rescuing an unconscious victim is a demanding procedure, and it might not be fast enough to save a life. Perhaps the most important lesson is to emphasize the seriousness of severe crevasse falls, and the value of a full-body harness. But as third man procedures become more widely known, perhaps lives will be saved.

COMPLICATIONS

At the Kahiltna Glacier airstrip, a party of sixteen climbers divided themselves into rope teams of four. They loaded their packs and sleds, and readied their chest harnesses, ropes, and prusiks. This day in late June was the first in their quest to climb Denali, the highest peak in North America. They embarked at about 7:30 p.m., a time when snow conditions were sloppy, but the coming twilight would gradually firm the surface. Two and one-half hours up the glacier, the second member of the lead team broke through a snowbridge. She and her sled fell in about four meters, giving both of her adjacent teammates a strong yank, but one they held by ice-ax arrest.

Within minutes, a member from another rope team was belayed out to the hole, where he heard her give a faint cry for help. They immediately built a Z-pulley system onto her rope, and began to haul. Quickly the hauling got difficult, then impossible; she was being hauled into the overhanging lip. A member was belayed out the unstable eave. He saw the woman unconscious, her spine arched back from her tie-in. Her sled, which may have clubbed her in the fall, still hung free from her harness and her pack was still on.

As the man reached to free her, the lip gave way, and he fell a couple meters onto his belay. From there he cut away her sled and pack, and tied a new rope onto her harness. With this rope the team hauled again, and hauled harder. She was still embedded in the lip. With a dozen or so people heaving, suddenly the line went slack. The woman's harness loop proved to be the weak point of an over-stressed system; it broke and she dropped to the bottom.

At this point another team came along, and one of them was lowered into the vault. He found the woman and tied a rope to her. Then, as the others hauled, he guided her over the lip. But it was too late; the woman had died.

Here was a team with a moderate level of preparation, certainly more prepared than many who make their way up Denali. Nevertheless, they found themselves unprepared for a dire situation, not knowing the importance of attaching sleds to the climbing rope, of freeing the victim from a load, of descending to assist a struggling victim, or the severity of an overhanging lip.

CHAPTER 5
SKIING AND HAULING SLEDS

Skis and sleds allow parties to cover more ground and carry more weight. But they also throw new factors into glacier travel and crevasse rescue.

GLACIER SKIING

Traveling on skis gives the obvious benefit of spreading your body weight over a greater surface area, making you less likely to fall through a snow-bridge. The increase in surface area is about six to ninefold, although this does not make you six to nine times less likely to fall through. The bridging effectiveness of skis varies with a number of factors, including the direction the ski's point relative to the crevasse and what type of snow is present. But clearly the greater surface area and greater bridging ability of skis make them a safety item, especially when traveling uphill.

Of course, the joy and real efficiency in skis comes from traveling downhill. And, unfortunately, skiing downhill and safeguarding against crevasse falls are not very compatible. Even the best skiers should hold no illusions about trying to link turns while roped to a partner who's trying to do the same, while both are looking out for and avoiding crevasses. Many people try it once, and find out that they're *more* likely to get pulled off into a crevasse. Therefore, skiing downhill while roped for glacier travel means, at best, skidding along in a measured snowplow, perhaps cutting an occasional christy to change direction. The better skier should ski behind, because he or she adjusts to the pace of the skier ahead to keep a minimum of slack in the rope. To keep the pace slow and stay in control, many people keep their skins on. Skiers should have runaway straps to keep a released ski from disappearing into a crevasse.

◀ *Skiing up a glacier on Mount Baker, North Cascades (Courtesy Ace Kvale)*

The other problem with skiing uphill or downhill in crevassed terrain is holding a fall. When one member crosses a known crevasse, the adjacent member can turn his or her skis sideways to the potential pull, to better resist a fall. But in any serious fall adjacent members will be pulled off their feet. For this reason, ski poles should be rigged with ice-ax arrest grips. Another option is to wrap an ice ax to one of the poles using duct tape. For getting out of a crevasse, one should make arrangements to remove skis and attach them to the pack.

Some people feel that the added surface area provided with skis makes crevasse falls unlikely enough that they can dispense with a rope. While it's indisputable that skis help, no one can make this judgment absolutely, and it's easy to base the judgment more on a desire to have fun than on the glacier's conditions. On Oregon's Mount Hood, a cohort of mine was linking telemarks down an apparently crevasse-free snow slope, and he carved one right into a covered slot, plunging parallel to the walls for 50 feet. Amazingly, he suffered only minor injuries and his buddies were able to rescue him.

A party can easily be tempted to ski downhill unroped if they have skied up a glacier as a rope team, checking out the best route and general snowbridge conditions. If everything seems safe enough, they can ski down with more confidence, roping up where prudent. Even with this prior inspection, though, ski parties tend to skew their judgment because once the skis are pointing down, the temptation to value fun over safety can be great. Also, snowbridges generally weaken as a day progresses, and bridges that seemed fine on the morning climb can fail during the afternoon descent.

Snowshoes also reduce your chances of breaking through a snowbridge, although their surface area and bridging length are significantly less than with skis. There's no problem controlling a downhill plod with snowshoes, though, so for those less skilled at skiing or who are carrying a large pack or sled, snowshoes can be a smart compromise.

HAULING SLEDS

Other than traveling unroped, there's probably nothing a glacier traveler can do to make crevasse falls more dangerous than to haul a sled. We might marvel at how much easier it is to haul a 60-pound expedition load on a sled than in a backpack, but in a crevasse fall that sled plunges in right after you. And when the rope brings you to a halt, those 60 pounds plummet onto you with a deadly force. In recent years, at least two crevasse deaths on Denali can be partly or largely attributed to sleds.

The basic preventive to sled slayings is to attach the sled to the climbing rope behind you. This way, as the rope comes taut, the sled will halt and stay suspended above you in the crevasse. No system for setting this up has been devised that offers all the safety and convenience we'd like, but the best system is a pretty good compromise.

Most people on typical budgets get by with the inexpensive plastic sleds designed for kids' snow frolics. Haul poles of aluminum, conduit, or PVC can be improvised onto them for better downhill and side-hill control. Commercial sleds with rigid haul poles are nice, but they don't prevent the load from crashing onto you. Another good option is to drag a haul bag made of smooth, heavy fabric.

In any case, it's most comfortable to haul a sled with a separate haul line clipped to a carabiner on the back of your pack. Attach the sled to the climbing rope with a three-wrap prusik on the sled's trailing end. Adjust the prusik along the climbing rope so that when you're traveling and the haul rope is taut, the climbing rope has an absolute minimum of slack (see fig. 5.1). You don't want the climbing rope so taut that you're hauling the sled with it, but you also don't want it so slack that you hang from the sled's haul line when you fall through. It's wise to load gear into a strong duffel and attach the prusik to a strong loop on the duffel, not to the sled's plastic, which could rip under the stress of a fall.

If you have the appropriate minimum of slack in this system, when you do punch through a snowbridge most of your weight goes onto the

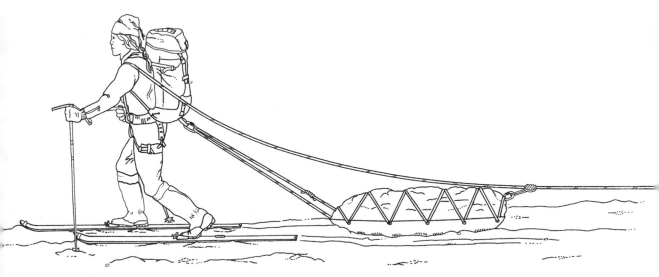

Figure 5.1 Glacier travel with a sled

climbing rope, because the stretch and play in the prusik sink the sled toward you just enough to take tension off the haul line. Thus you hang from your seat harness as without a sled (see fig. 5.2), and when you remove your pack you also detach yourself from the sled.

Figure 5.2 *In a crevasse with a sled*

To ascend out of the crevasse past the sled's prusik, you need a spare prusik (or an ascender that goes on and off the rope easily) and a spare harness carabiner. With the Texas prusik system you simply ascend to the sled's prusik, wrap your spare prusik on the climbing rope above the sled's prusik, stand tall to clip this new prusik into your spare locking carabiner, and unclip the original prusik. When you rise up enough to hang from the new waist prusik, take your feet out of the stirrups and rewrap the stirrup prusik above the sled's prusik. If you use ascenders, make sure that both ascenders attach to your seat harness, and when you reach the sled's prusik, replace the ascenders one at a time above the prusik. If the sled is heavy, you will need to untie from the climbing rope to continue. It is best to get a belay from your partners above.

Should a victim with a sled need to be hauled out, you'll want to send down a new strand to haul on, one without a sled attached to it. After being hauled a short distance, the victim can untie from the original rope, and the sled can be hauled up later.

Another problem with sleds is dragging them downhill and along side hills, for they slide and roll downslope at their own whim, paying no heed to their owner's most fervent demands and sometimes threatening to drag the owner away. Clipping a sled into the glacier travel rope can help solve these problems, for the climber behind can help brake and even steer the sled. To aid in this you can clip clove hitches in the climbing rope in front and behind the sled, adjusting the hitches so there's slight tension between them across the top of the sled. When descending, the member behind brakes the sled with the climbing rope, keeping it from crashing into the partner's legs. Another aid for downhill travel is to run a knotted cord under the sled's belly as a friction brake, tying it at both bow and stern.

To keep the sled from swinging downslope while traversing a side hill, the member behind keeps tension on the climbing rope, and this tension holds the sled in line with the direction of travel especially with double-clove hitches on the sled. Though the member ahead is now pulling against this tension, and coordination between the two members needs to be close, this is far better than having the sled slide, flip, and pull downslope. Another consideration, though, is that the clove hitches in the climbing rope will be impossible to untie should the rope be tensioned with the weight of someone who's fallen in a crevasse, and this will make it impossible to haul the victim out on that rope. For this reason, it's wise to tie-in the sled with clove hitches only when another rope or rope team is available.

You may have noticed that all these precautions and improvements can't be applied to the last person in a rope team, who has no one behind to keep a sled in line. Basically, a team has two unsavory options for the last person. The first is not to give that person a sled and distribute that load among the other members. The second is to give the last person a sled and travel very cautiously, clipping the sled to the rope ahead when crossing treacherous bridges.

Al Pack on Shafat Glacier, Nun, Kashmir

THE GAME OF CREVASSE ROULETTE

As mentioned in the introduction, a party's style of glacier travel generally reflects its attitudes. People go into glaciated areas pretty sure about how much risk they are willing to take to complete their endeavor. As they perceive various degrees of hazard they adjust their procedures to maintain that acceptable level of risk.

But since the crevasse hazard can never be gauged precisely, glacier travel is always a gamble that a party's precautions will match up with the actual hazard. Not only is it difficult to know just where crevasses lie and how strong their bridges are, it's even harder to predict how severe a crevasse fall might be and what the extrication might involve. Thus, when a party settles on procedures such as the number of rope teams, how to cross what bridges at what time of day, how many anchors to carry and so on, they can't know exactly what they're preparing for. To emphasize this uncertainty, we can think of glacier travel as a kind of crevasse roulette, a game of chance in which the percentage of unlucky spins of the wheel is never sure.

The object of crevasse roulette is to travel on a glacier with the minimum of gear and rigamarole, while keeping the chances of dying in a crevasse as small as possible.

When confronted with this metaphor for glacier travel, most of us say we'd like to play the game at a fairly conservative level. That is, we like the security of being able to rescue ourselves from the worst-case scenario—falling a good distance into a crevasse to a free-hanging stop, perhaps with injuries. This we want beyond the relative security of knowing we will usually avoid that worst-case scenario in the first place.

A major reason we want such safety is because we see crevasses as an unglamorous risk, not worth tempting fate for—in contrast to, say, scaling a peak. Unfortunately, this same "not worth risking" attitude too often includes "not worth hassling for." This "nuisance" view of the crevasse hazard dilutes our interest in giving ourselves the safety we desire. We rope up but don't carry or don't know how to use anchors or prusiks; we carry heavy packs without chest harnesses; we travel with yards of slack rope between us.

In this way, it seems that because crevasses generally are not hazards inherent to "climbing," because the odds of falling through a weak bridge are irregular, and because many glacier excursions are incident-free, we don't view crevasses with the same wary eye as we do other climbing hazards like falling, fatigue, or even avalanches and rockfall. We forget that a single crevasse fall can become the major issue of a mountaineering endeavor. With the hazards not well thought out, our perception of playing crevasse roulette at a conservative level becomes a pleasant illusion compared to our real odds.

Most people who have died in crevasses were climbing unroped, and the overwhelming majority of those people were surprised—they were either naive about the risk or they denied the risk they knew. We can guess that most who've died while climbing roped assumed that the precautions they were taking were adequate to save them from the fatal situation. Very few went out fully aware of the risk and fully ready to take it.

This is not to say that we should travel glaciers with the least possible risk—which would be to anchor-belay every step. Our goal is to play crevasse roulette at a level of risk as close to our choosing as possible.

When we have an intimate knowledge of and intuition for crevasses and snowbridges, we can play at a more informed, aware level. When we know how to avoid the worst case and how to rescue from it, we can play at whatever level we want, up to the conservative level that most people desire.

We all know that one person's acceptable risk is another's suicide mission and yet another's confining security blanket—it's important that we preserve this freedom to climb in the style we choose. Just as important is to accept full responsibility for whatever style we choose. The crucial task is not eliminating risk, but knowing more clearly just what risks we take, and just how effectively our precautions will serve us. Given this knowledge, glacier travelers almost always make prudent choices.

Experienced glacier travelers know the stakes are high, and relative security from crevasse death comes with precious little investment. An experienced party on a typical alpine glacier can be quite secure with just a pound or two of gear they wouldn't carry anyway, and perhaps 15 minutes of added procedure. Mostly it's the weightless, time-free items—awareness and ability—that are our best investments, for in crevasse roulette they both reduce the hassle and improve the odds.

"Negotiating the countless stretchmarks on a large Alaskan glacier is often the most vexing and frightening aspect of a mountain adventure."

—Fred Beckey. From *Alaska Ascents*,
1996. Bill Sherwonit, Ed.

REMOTENESS

From the top of Good Neighbor Peak, the 15,600-foot east summit of Mount Vancouver, two very experienced climbers looked over much of the Saint Elias Range, one of the world's great ice wildernesses. They started a half-mile ridge-walk to the main summit, but midway across a harsh wind with a scud signaled a storm, then one member started feeling altitude sickness. They ducked down Vancouver's northwest ridge to a campsite at 12,500 feet. Here they waited out a windy day of storm.

When the tempest eased they broke camp and reinstalled themselves at the one-third points along their 50-meter rope. Although they were on a high ridge they took precautions for crevasses with prusiks on the rope, anchors and pulleys handy, and they traveled with the rope extended. Wearing crampons on the wind-hardened snow, they crested a subsidiary summit on this ridge, and the first climber walked across a bridge near the end of an obvious crevasse. The second followed in his prints, but the steps broke through and dropped the climber in to his knees. He shouted, and as his partner turned around the bridge failed completely.

After a 10-foot drop, one of the climber's crampons caught on the wall of the crevasse and flipped him upside-down. The rope ran somewhat oblique to the crevasse wall, and so he swung and kept falling upside-down, dragging his partner, in ice-ax arrest, toward the lip. When the arrest finally held, the falling climber was flipped upright by his full-body harness. He shrieked with pain from his lower leg because it felt like someone was pouring boiling water into it. He was 40 feet down, with severe artery and muscle damage, and his leg was filling with blood.

He'd been traveling with a sling ready on his pack and with this he got the load off his back and onto the rope. A few feet away there was a block of ice wedged between the walls of the crevasse, and he pulled himself over to rest on that. With the rope no longer weighted, the partner above was free to set an anchor, which he did by burying his entire pack in the dry snow. Then he belayed himself with a prusik out to the lip. His partner yelled up that he would like his pack hauled, and this was accomplished.

The victim decided that prusiking could further traumatize his leg, but feeling like a trapped animal he wanted to start getting out right away. He felt that with a tight belay and two ice tools he could climb the Styrofoam-wall of the crevasse and keep his damaged leg out of harm. So with tension from the belay he heaved and hopped up the crevasse wall, to where the upper wall overhung with an eave of loose snow. He made some more progress by clearing away scoops from the overhang, but more tricks were needed. The surface climber tied off the belay and sent down the other end of the rope with a series of loops tied into it. With this the fallen climber climbed up another couple feet. Then he just held tight as his partner heaved him the last meter.

He was shivering from cold, shock, and adrenaline, so they immediately set up their tent and assessed the damage. Although they shrank at the thought of the 7,000-foot descent and then 20-plus miles of valley glacier to their base camp, they were grateful for every bit of crevasse preparation they had made.

The next day they splinted the leg and started down. Easy ground was torture for the injured man, but on steep ground he could be lowered on the rope, though this meant that the healthy man suffered the hazard of circumventing the steep area alone and unroped. One time the injured man was lowered out of view into another crevasse, requiring another extrication. Down on the valley glacier, the man limped as best he could, mostly in exquisite pain. Too often a breaking crust would hyperextend the damaged leg, and convulsing agony would send his body into spastic somersaults. It took them five days of belabored travel to reach their base camp on the Seward Glacier. Two days after that a plane retrieved them for the trip home.

APPENDIX 1

RESCUE PRACTICE SESSIONS

One of the paradoxes of glacier travel is that safe, uneventful trips do not prepare you for the eventuality of crevasse rescue. Therefore, competence at crevasse rescue demands setting up practice sessions on a glacier.

It's usually more convenient to first practice on a crevasse in a glacier's ablation zone. Here, on the icy lower reaches, you don't have to worry about genuine crevasse falls before you've learned how to rescue people from them, the anchors in ice are safer, and you don't have to worry about genuine lip problems.

First, find a flat area with a nice deep crevasse. Set up bombproof anchors and lower a mock victim into the crevasse with a belay device. (The "victim" can be a pack full of gear or snow instead of a person.) He or she or it should go down tied to the end of another rope, which becomes the rescue/haul rope. Once the victim is a good distance into the crevasse, set another bombproof anchor, pull the rescue rope taut, connect it to the anchor with a prusik, and commence rescue procedures. As you haul the victim up, someone takes up the original lowering rope as a backup belay.

To practice prusiking, have your partner lower you with a brake on the anchor and tie off the belay. Then prusik out on the same rope.

Once your group is practiced at rescue procedures, it's a good idea to head up to the snow-covered reaches of a glacier and practice in more genuine conditions. Here again, choose your practice site carefully; try to find a flat work area next to a good crevasse with at most a modest eave of snow. You don't want to walk onto a huge, unstable marquee that might require the adrenaline of a genuine rescue to get back over. If you're in the Cascades in July or August you should have no problem finding a suitable crevasse, but if you're in the Alaska Range you might just decide to stay out of as many crevasses as possible. Again, set bombproof anchors and lower a mock victim, then haul out on another set of anchors.

APPENDIX 2

SOME USEFUL IMPROVISATIONS

Here are three additional tricks that can come in handy.

KIWI COIL TIE-IN

Guides in New Zealand have developed a method for people to tie in at the end of a rope that wraps coils around the shoulder to offer reasonable torso support. Overseas it has been termed the kiwi coil.

1. Start by tying the end of the rope into your seat harness as usual; then wrap coils from the shoulder and under the other arm. Wrap the coils so they reach just to the bottom of your rib cage (see fig. A.1a). If you're at one end of a three- or four-person rope team, wrap about five coils. If you're one of a two-person rope team, wrap enough coils to take up the amount of rope you need to reach your partner (see "Two-Person Parties" in chapter 2).

2. When you have enough coils wrapped, make a bight in the rope as it comes from under your arm, and pass it under the original knotted strand and then under all the coils. Then with this bight, tie an overhand on a bight around both the original knotted strand and the strand going out to your partner.

3. Clip the knotted bight into doubled carabiners on your seat harness. When you hang from this tie-in, most of your weight should bear on the seat harness, with the coils reaching out from your torso somewhat, merely supporting your upper body. Test pull the rope to make sure that the seat harness will take its share of the weight, and retie the knot if necessary.

This method shortens the span between climbers and ensures some free rope on the ends, so all the advantages and disadvantages of shorter spans apply. If you plan to wear a heavy pack with this method, test hang

Figure A.1a A kiwi coil tie-in: wrap coils around shoulder and under arm

Figure A.1b A kiwi coil tie-in: use bight to tie overhand knot around coils

Figure A.1c A kiwi coil tie-in: clip bight into carabiner on seat harness

with it first to make sure you will have enough support from the coils in a crevasse.

KLEIMHEIST WEBBING "PRUSIK"

With a runner of 1-inch or 9/16-inch webbing you can improvise a prusik by tying it around a climbing rope in a kleimheist knot. Hold an open bight of the webbing free, and wrap it down the rope barber-pole style, making three to four wraps. Then feed the tail back up through the bight you've held open (see fig. A.2), pull the tail back down, and the kleimheist is complete. This can be used anywhere a prusik is used, except as a ratchet at the anchor of a hauling system.

BACHMAN KNOT

Familiar to Europeans, the Bachman knot is a prusik-type knot that actually performs better than the tried-and-true prusik. With its wraps cinching around a carabiner's spine as well as the climbing rope, the Bachman grabs at least as tightly as a prusik, yet once the load is removed it slides more readily. The carabiner also adds a convenient handle for moving the

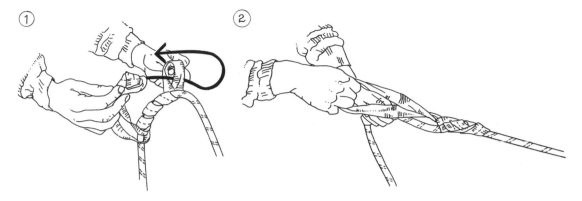

Figure A.2 (left) Kleimheist knot tied with 1-inch webbing: top, wrap bight down rope barber-pole style; (right) feed tail back through bight

unweighted knot, although you cannot pull on the carabiner and expect the knot to grip.

To tie the Bachman, simply clip a prusik loop onto a carabiner, and then wrap the doubled cord around both the climbing rope and the spine of the carabiner, working down the carabiner barber-pole style. Three wraps will usually suffice, depending on the diameter of the rope. The Bachman grabs when you load the remaining loop; unweighted, it slides when you push or pull the wraps and carabiner directly. The Bachman knot can be used anywhere a prusik would be used, except that it will take a load only in the direction it was tied for; unlike a prusik, it is not bi-directional, therefore, it is not recommended for a self-belay.

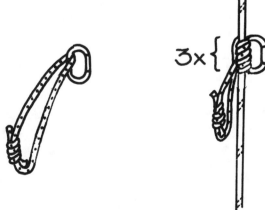

Figure A.3 Bachman knot

INDEX

ABOUT THE MOUNTAINEERS

Founded in 1906, The Mountaineers is a Seattle-based non-profit outdoor activity and conservation club with 15,000 members, whose mission is "to explore, study, preserve, and enjoy the natural beauty of the outdoors ...." The club sponsors many classes and year-round outdoor activities in the Pacific Northwest, and supports environmental causes by sponsoring legislation and presenting educational programs. The Mountaineers Books supports the club's mission by publishing travel and natural history guides, instructional texts, and works on conservation and history. For information, call or write The Mountaineers, Club Headquarters, 300 Third Avenue West, Seattle, Washington, 98119; (206) 284-6310.

Send or call for our catalog of more than 300 outdoor titles:

The Mountaineers Books
1001 SW Klickitat Way, Suite 201
Seattle, WA 98134
800-553-4453
mbooks@mountaineers.org
www.mountaineersbooks.org

ABOUT THE AUTHOR

Andy Selters has climbed all over North America, Asia, and Peru, and is the author of four other mountain guidebooks and numerous mountaineering articles. During his years as a guide and trainer for the American Alpine Institute in Bellingham, Washington, Selters observed a need for updated literature on glacier travel and crevasse rescue, from which this guidebook sprang. He now lives in Bishop, California.

(Photo by Deb Martin)